Praise for **HEALING BIG HURTS**

"This is the first book I've encountered that truly addresses *how* parents can be meaningfully involved in their child's trauma therapy—and what that process requires of them physically, emotionally, and relationally. As an attachment and trauma-informed therapist, I've long advocated for parental involvement in their child's therapy, but this book goes deeper than any other resource, offering practical, compassionate guidance for navigating the emotional challenges and opportunities that come with that involvement. *Healing Big Hurts* should be in the hands of every parent whose child has experienced trauma and on the shelf of every therapist who works with children and families. It fills a long-standing gap in trauma literature with empathy, expertise, and actionable guidance."

—**Karen Doyle Buckwalter, MSW, LCSW, RPT-S™**, certified Theraplay® trainer and supervisor, coauthor of *Raising the Challenging Child: How to Minimize Meltdowns, Reduce Conflict, and Increase Cooperation*

"This is a very important book, a gold mine of information and inspiration. It is a book I wish I'd had available to me years ago as I was learning 'on the job' how to co-parent a blended family with copious emotional needs. It is beautifully organized and written, and, most importantly, it brings the parent/caregiver into the heart of the therapy, rather than on the periphery. It is a detailed map of the experience of parenting a child who is involved in the therapeutic journey, specifically trauma therapy. I highly recommend this book to parents, caregivers, and therapists alike."

—**Andrew Seubert, LMHC, NCC,** EMDRIA-approved trainer for clinicians, author of *The Courage to Feel: A Practical Guide to the Power and Freedom of Emotional Honesty* and *How Simon Left His Shell: The Courage to Feel for Young People*

"This book is a formidable antidote to the feelings of helplessness, isolation, and exhaustion experienced by parents who desperately wish to play an active role in their child's therapeutic journey to overcome the invisible wounds inflicted by early trauma. For it is mistaken to believe that a wee human can magically be 'resilient' and psychologically rebuild themselves alone after individual therapeutic care and without the solid, warm, and determined presence of one or several attachment figures. In these pages, you will find accessible scientific tools and discover how, in addition to playing your irreplaceable role as a parent, you can also become a true resilience mentor for your child."

—**Johanne Lemieux,** social worker, psychotherapist, and author of books on adoptive parenting

"Oh, how I wish this book had been available throughout my 40-year career of working with children who have big hurts. The authors have created an excellent, essential resource for parents and therapists trying their best to support healing within traumatized children."

—**Nita Baer, MA,** certified Lifespan Integration therapist and consultant

"Sometimes it's hard for families to remember what counselors have explained in therapy sessions. This book serves as an indispensable resource for its abundance of valuable counseling information, which can be difficult to recall and apply accurately in the middle of a specific family need."

—**Kirstin Simpson,** adoptive parent, forensic nurse examiner, and forensic nursing services consultant

"This is a must-have resource, not only for every parent/caregiver who is wanting to help their child navigate the road of trauma counseling, but also for any professional seeking a better understanding of the process of trauma healing. As an adoptive parent, I wish I'd had access to a book like this right from the start. Chatwin and VanDiermen have created an easily understandable, knowledge-rich resource that explains the whole counseling process and what the parent's role needs to be. *Healing Big Hurts* is filled with practical advice and helpful stories. It is thoroughly user friendly and accessible to anyone. I highly recommend this wonderful resource to everyone involved in the process of bringing healing to our traumatized children."

—**Kaisu Aldom,** adoptive parent and author of *Refuge in the Shadows: Searching for Caring Community in the Midst of Trauma*

HEALING BIG HURTS

Understanding Your Role in Your Child's Trauma Therapy

A Supportive Guide for Parents & Caregivers

Andrea Chatwin, MA, CCC, and
Meagan VanDiermen, MA, RCC

HEALING BIG HURTS

Copyright © 2025 by Andrea Chatwin & Meagan VanDiermen

Published by
PESI Publishing, Inc.
3839 White Ave
Eau Claire, WI 54703

Cover and interior design by Emily Dyer
Editing by Jenessa Jackson

ISBN 9781683738619 (print)
ISBN 9781683738626 (ePUB)
ISBN 9781683738633 (ePDF)

All rights reserved.
Printed in the United States of America.

TABLE OF CONTENTS

Introduction ix

1. Understanding Trauma and Trauma Therapy for Kids 1
2. How We Provide Trauma Therapy to Children with Attachment Losses 19
3. When You Need to Do Your Own Work 31
4. A Parent's Role in Trauma Therapy 47
5. Choosing the Best Therapist for Your Child 59
6. Engaging Your Child in the *Why* and *What* Explanation of Therapy 75
7. The Parent-Therapist Alliance 87
8. Setting the Relational Foundation for Effective Therapy 101
9. Preparing for the Impact of Therapy on Family Life 117
10. Understanding the Process: What Happens in Trauma Therapy 129
11. Preparing for the Commitment of Therapy 141
12. Managing Your Own Reactions in Session 155
13. Noticing Your Child's Overwhelm 167
14. Making Informed Decisions: Trauma Therapy and Complementary Interventions 183

Conclusion 193

References 195

Appendix A: Using Timelines to Understand
               Complex Behaviors 197

Appendix B: A Story About Going to Therapy 198

Appendix C: Daily Noticing Checklist 201

Appendix D: Erikson's Stages of Development 203

About the Authors 205

INTRODUCTION

ealing Big Hurts is a road map that helps parents navigate the journey of trauma therapy for their child or teenager, with us as the guides to help you stay the course. We'll be along for the ride from beginning to end, with all the stops in between, on this challenging journey. You can read this guide from cover to cover or explore what is most relevant to you right now. Either way, we anticipate you will refer to this book repeatedly, reminding yourself of the *whys* and *hows* when things get hard. As your support system, we want more than anything to help you feel seen, understood, coached, comforted, and celebrated as you do the hard work of being a parent participating in trauma therapy with your child.

You Are the Missing Piece of Child Therapy

Traditional trauma interventions for children and youth don't put a lot of emphasis on the role of parents or attachment figures in the therapy process. Instead, they focus on the child's relationship with the therapist, anticipating that the combination of that relationship and the therapist's expertise will lead to healing and change. However, we have discovered along the way that many youth who have experienced early trauma and relational loss—and especially those who have gone through multiple caregivers—tend to arrive for therapy without a secure attachment relationship. In this case, the therapist can easily be seen as a viable option for attachment given their ability to attune, read cues, and empathize deeply.

Unfortunately, when the child feels or believes that their therapist understands their thoughts and feelings better than their parents do, it sets them up to feel alone in their daily life, as though only a professional can support them. We also risk the possibility that the therapist will change offices, discontinue services, or simply be so busy that frequent sessions are difficult to access. These circumstances can leave the child feeling indefinitely disconnected. After witnessing this dynamic and the devastating outcomes that resulted, we decided to change the way we practice. We made a dramatic—and at the time very unpopular—decision in our clinical practice to prioritize developing a secure attachment between the parent and child in order for it to be the foundation for all other healing work to build from.

After practicing this way for many years, we now know without a doubt that kids with early attachment losses benefit from an attachment figure who attends and is actively engaged in trauma therapy. This new therapeutic approach underscores the importance of first establishing one key attachment relationship—the parent-child relationship—as the cornerstone for healthy development. The therapist operates as the facilitator of the healing process, serving as a guide for the parent, a safe base for the child-parent dyad, and a thermostat for the counseling space. Parents provide the container the child needs within which they can explore the big hurts that would otherwise remain deeply buried. So, if you are a parent, guardian, or alternate attachment figure caring for a child with trauma, *you* are the key to creating enough emotional safety and security to support effective healing through trauma therapy.

Introduction

Why We Wrote This Book

We wrote this book to translate our years of clinical experience into a parent guide that will allow you to feel equipped to navigate trauma therapy with your child. From the first step of finding a therapist to the ongoing path of continuing the work at home, this guide will give you everything you need to feel calm and confident about embarking on this journey with your child.

My coauthor, Meagan VanDiermen, and I, Andrea Chatwin, have been supporting foster families, adoptive families, next-of-kin families, and reunified families through trauma therapy for over thirteen years. When we first met, I had recently become an adoptive parent and was working in a mental health clinic as an early childhood specialist. Meagan was finishing up her master's degree in counseling psychology and embarking on her own parenting journey. From our first conversation, I knew that Meagan had that "special thing"—that quality you need to be a good trauma therapist. It's hard to describe what I mean by that because I just *know* it when I see it. The best word to describe what Meagan has is a deep sense of *knowing* when she is in the same room as someone who is hurting. At the time, I recognized this was someone I wanted to work with long term, and together we began shifting the way that children and families impacted by significant trauma received therapeutic care.

Simultaneously, I was learning what it was like to *be* the parent of a child with significant trauma. My first daughter started her life without the necessities of connection and attachment to a primary caregiver. She suffered the most significant loss a child can experience: separation from her biological mother, father, siblings, extended family, and community. Her body carried with her the memories of that loss, as well as the subsequent disorganization that comes from having your basic needs met by *multiple* caregivers instead of one stable caregiver. My journey to meet her needs provided a level of insight that my work thus far had not been able to do. As she grew, developed, and began to learn about herself, she, too, benefited from therapy, and I experienced sitting in the parent's seat watching her process the impact of those early losses on her body and brain.

Years later, when my second daughter joined our family as a teenager, I struggled and failed to find a therapist who understood the importance of parent involvement in child trauma therapy. I experienced what it was like to take my teenage daughter to her appointments, wait in the car, and feel an incredible sense of helplessness to support her through the process. As we were working hard day in and day out to build trust, connection, and a parent-child relationship, she was also building a strong relationship with her therapist. A tension developed between these two relationships, with no understanding of the way each was working for or against the other. This was a difficult time in my parenting journey, and it strengthened my resolve to provide families with the opportunity to access therapy that builds attachment security and resolves trauma simultaneously.

Meagan and I have felt the pull toward writing this book for several years now. We want to demystify the process of trauma counseling for children and youth and offer parents and professionals a guide for strengthening attachment by engaging parents in trauma therapy. We also want to give you as many practical tools as possible to help you feel ready, engaged, and self-assured in your role as a parent or caregiver. Most importantly, we want to support you through this incredibly emotional experience by discussing *ahead of time* the common thoughts, feelings, and behaviors you may find yourself having along the way. Knowledge is power, and knowing what to expect and how to respond means that you can breathe deeply and engage fully throughout the process.

Introduction

Whom This Book Was Written For

This book is for you: the parent, family member, primary caregiver, guardian, or chosen attachment figure who is putting their heart and soul into parenting a child who has experienced trauma and attachment losses. You were our primary consideration in writing this book. We wanted it to feel practical, supportive, easy to understand, and comforting. Think of this book as your always-present partner in a process that can at times feel lonely and overwhelming. You decide how you engage with this book, so monitor your reactions, nurture yourself along the way, and take it at the speed that feels good for you. It's really the perfect conversation because *you* tell us when you've had enough for now. Just close us up and walk away until you are ready to engage again.

If you are a trauma therapist, you will find *Healing Big Hurts* to be an essential guidebook for engaging and harnessing the power of parent involvement in trauma therapy. Everything you need to know—from that first inquiry about your services to that conversation about closure—is in this book. Our collective experiences have been poured into creating the language and processes needed to engage kids in therapy, including determining when and how to include parents, setting parents up for success in the room, handling conflicting stories, and addressing complex dynamics between parents and children during sessions.

If you are a social worker or other decision-maker for children in government care, this book will help you learn about the ins and outs of child trauma therapy and the role of the parent or caregiver in every step of the process. It will also help you feel equipped to make recommendations about when and with whom children in government care should engage in trauma therapy. We hope it encourages you to take an active role in the therapeutic process for the kids you are responsible for and that it helps you feel comfortable asking questions about the therapeutic modality being used, the expected time frame for treatment, the potential complications, and the necessary supports you need to put in place for therapy to be effective. We also hope this book offers a deeper understanding of the impact that trauma therapy can have on the entire family. We know that what impacts one person in a family system has ripple effects on other family members and the system in its entirety. What we see consistently in our work is that trauma and the process of healing from trauma deeply impact family systems.

If you are a parent, we highly suggest that you read this book along with at least one other person or, better yet, a small group of people. If you are part of a parenting partnership and you want to be on the same page as your partner, it would be ideal if you read it together. We know schedules are busy, so this may mean that each of you reads a chapter at a time on your own and you then find a few minutes to discuss it with each other. We find that there is typically one parent who carries more of the emotional load when it comes to supporting trauma therapy, and this is one way to ensure that each caregiver has the same level of knowledge about the process. As the parent who is carrying the heavier load, you will need some understanding of the way this process impacts you and, oftentimes, the work you will be doing to resolve your own trauma. If you are a parent who is not directly involved in sessions, having a reading partner will help you feel connected to the process and allow you to understand what is happening both within and outside of sessions.

Another option is to connect with other parents who are also raising children with a history of early trauma. Learning about this process and supporting each other along the way is an amazing opportunity to lean in to your community. Other parents who "get it" are one of your best resources on this journey. If there is no obvious group of participants to engage with, consider starting your own group, or connect with a local agency that can promote the idea of this book group among parents in similar situations.

Introduction

What You Will Find Inside

While we believe that the greatest benefit of this book comes from reading it cover to cover, we recognize that anyone parenting a child with trauma may already be feeling overwhelmed. Therefore, we separated the information into clearly defined chapters so that you can go directly to the parts of the book that feel the most relevant for you at the time. Chapters 1 through 6 cover the initial steps you'll need to take in the treatment process, such as learning about trauma, doing your own inner work, choosing the best therapist for your child, and introducing your child to therapy. If you have already started treatment and feel confident that your child understands why they are in therapy and why you are there with them—and you believe your therapist is a good fit for your family—you may want to skip ahead to chapter 7, which focuses on building the parent-therapist alliance. You can then read chapters 8 through 14 to learn how to better navigate the process of trauma therapy, including how to prep other family members, overcome obstacles to involvement, manage the pace of sessions, navigate shifting priorities, and more. This information is also helpful to review if your child changes therapists or if another child in your family begins treatment.

    As therapists, we know the power of stories, so woven throughout the book are stories of families who have already made the journey of trauma therapy, and their experiences light the way for you to see what life can be like on the other side. All the names and identifying information in these stories have been changed to protect privacy, but you will feel moved by the struggles, the joys, and the ways life can be lived with more ease on the other side of trauma therapy.

    We have packed as much into this book as possible so you can feel confident about every aspect of treatment, whether that involves knowing how to explain trauma therapy to children at different ages and developmental stages or discovering what you need to do in your own therapeutic work. There is also a great deal of content about what you can expect in your own brain, body, and relationships as you support your child in exploring their big hurts. No matter where you are on this journey, we hope that you feel us cheering you on from the sidelines as you walk this pathway to healing with your child.

CHAPTER 1

Understanding Trauma and Trauma Therapy for Kids

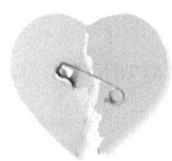

If you are a parent reading this book, we can assume that you are committed to helping your kid enjoy their childhood and have all the wonderful experiences that this time of their life can bring. You have probably also seen firsthand the way that traumatic experiences can interfere with both the joyful parts and the learning parts of growing up. You want to give your child the best opportunity to heal from the early experiences that have interfered with their ability to navigate the world, interact with others, and see themself. In this first chapter, we are going to walk you through everything you need to develop a strong knowledge base around trauma, including the different types of trauma, its impacts on the body and brain, the process of healing, and the unique aspects of trauma therapy. With this increased information and understanding, you will feel better equipped as you begin this journey with your child.

What Is Trauma?

You may have noticed in recent years that the word *trauma* is used loosely in daily conversation among adults, teens, and even middle schoolers as they describe a wide variety of unexpected occurrences. It can be used humorously to lighten a heavy story or to give a dramatic flair when describing an unexpected event. Someone might even describe a particular life stress as "the trauma that never ends." The casualness of how this word is used can feel disarming to anyone who has stared into the heart and soul of a child suffering from unimaginable pain and loss. Therefore, when we use the word *trauma*, we are referring to the profound impact that certain experiences can have on a young child's developing brain and body. We have learned so much about the impact of trauma on development, and yet all around us, we see signs that there is more work to be done to ensure that children have a healthy start to life, allowing their brain and body to develop optimally.

Dr. Gabor Maté (2022) provides the most helpful way of explaining what trauma is so that we can differentiate between hard things that happen to kids and truly traumatic experiences: "Trauma is not what happens *to* you but what happens *inside* you" (p. 20). This means that one child may experience a multitude of stressful circumstances and negative life events but demonstrate only a few trauma symptoms or no symptoms at all. However, another child who experiences what might be considered "typical" childhood stressors may struggle well into adulthood with significant symptoms of trauma. Therefore, trauma is not necessarily a result of specific events or circumstances; it is a result of how someone *felt* when those things were happening. Did they feel alone or connected? Helpless or empowered? Supported or shamed?

This more nuanced definition of trauma helps parents remain open to understanding more than just what happened to their child. Knowing how trauma impacted their child's development—and the narrative their child holds about themself and their world—helps parents make sense of complex presentations. Bessel van der Kolk (2014) describes trauma well when he says, "Trauma, by definition, is unbearable and intolerable. [...] It takes tremendous energy to keep functioning while carrying the memory of terror, and the shame of utter weakness and vulnerability" (pp. 1–2).

Different Types of Traumas

There seems to be a great deal of inconsistency in the way major contributors to the field of trauma define what is considered traumatic. We particularly resonate with the way Dr. Bruce Perry and Oprah Winfrey (2021) differentiate between "big T" and "little t" forms of trauma. "Big T" traumas are major, life-threatening events that everyone would objectively agree are traumatic, such as natural disasters, violent crime, or a serious car accident. In contrast, "little t" traumas are cumulative life experiences that add up and manifest in the same ways that "big T" traumas do. These can include systemic experiences that create prolonged stress or that make someone lose hope, feel less safe, or feel differently about themself—for example, racism, bullying, divorce, financial difficulties, infidelity, and legal trouble. The authors wisely caution against anyone claiming that a particular experience or set of experiences is too small to be considered trauma.

In addition to these types of trauma, you might hear the term *single-incident trauma*, which refers to trauma that occurs only one time. Single-incident traumas can have a wide range of impacts depending on how the person felt after the event, how supported they were, and what their trauma history is. For example, consider a child without a history of trauma who gets into a car accident while driving with their family. If this child's parents work to create safety immediately after the incident and prior to future car rides, this child may not experience any lasting impact, and they may return to the way they functioned prior to the accident. However, if this is one of many scary experiences that the child has encountered—and if there was no attuned adult to create a sense of felt safety and to allow the child to express their emotional experience—this child may experience more wide-reaching effects. This is especially the case if the car accident is connected to previous memories of unprocessed trauma. In this case, the current trauma can act like a magnet, pulling other traumatic memories from the past back up, making it feel much heavier than a single traumatic event.

When a child is continually exposed to multiple, and often interrelated, forms of trauma, this is referred to as *developmental trauma* or *complex trauma*. Developmental trauma describes the impact of early repeated trauma and losses that happen within the child's important relationships, usually early in life (Lyons et al., 2020). This includes parental loss, multiple moves, family disruptions, and chronic stress or abuse. It is also possible for children in intact, stable families to experience developmental trauma due to external factors outside of the family's control, such as chronic medical procedures, community unrest, parental illness, and natural disasters. Developmental trauma can even start prior to birth if a pregnant mother is experiencing high levels of fear and stress, as her heightened cortisol and adrenaline levels can cross over into the placenta. This can impact an unborn child's experience of "feeling safe" inside the womb. Since the science of brain development tells us that a child's most critical period of development occurs between the prenatal period through age three, trauma that occurs during this time can have the most profound impact on functioning, affecting a child's ability to achieve developmental milestones and build secure attachment.

In contrast to developmental trauma, *complex trauma* can happen throughout the lifespan and be passed down from one generation to another. Complex trauma occurs when someone is exposed to multiple traumatic events, which are often of an invasive interpersonal nature. This can include domestic violence, chronic sexual abuse, profound neglect, or prolonged captivity. Complex trauma may not be visible to all those who have experienced it. Young people may walk around in the world functioning in a way that doesn't make them stand out—until they experience just one more trauma that overwhelms their system. The cumulative experiences of trauma across their lifespan may lead to a distinct difference between a child's chronological age and their developmental skills and abilities. For example, someone who is fifteen years old may have the social-emotional skills of an eight-year-old. You'll learn more about chronological versus developmental age later in this chapter.

When complex trauma is passed down across generations, either due to larger community experiences or familial experiences, it reflects what is known as *intergenerational* or *transgenerational trauma*. We don't have to look far for clear examples of transgenerational trauma. The Holocaust, the three-hundred-year enslavement of Black Americans, and the forced relocation of Indigenous families across North America (and mass attempts to eradicate their culture) are all examples of intergenerational trauma. In our community in particular, we see an overrepresentation of Indigenous children placed in government care, and those children carry in their bodies the impact of trauma inflicted on generations before them. The trauma is perpetuated by their removal from their family and culture.

Now that you have had an opportunity to read through the different definitions and types of trauma, we encourage you to take a moment to jot down a few thoughts on how these different types of traumas relate to your child and their experiences. We also suggest you do the same for yourself so that you might be more open to, and aware of, how trauma has impacted you. In later chapters, we will look more closely at how trauma impacts the developing brain and explore what interventions are supportive in healing these experiences.

How Trauma Impacts Functioning

The way trauma impacts functioning depends on a few different factors, the most significant being the timing of when it happens. If a child's trauma occurs in utero and during the first few years of life, the brain stem—which regulates many of the autonomic body functions—is significantly affected. As a result, involuntary physiological processes, such as blood pressure, heart rate, respiration, and digestion, are heavily impacted. This might present later as a child who struggles with hyperarousal, elevated heart rate, an inability to regulate body temperature, and difficulty with bowel movements. It makes sense why this would happen: Kids whose brains were formed under duress may spend a lifetime working at regulating these involuntary systems.

Similarly, trauma that occurs during specific developmental milestones, such as walking, feeding, toileting, or talking, may cause delays or atypical outcomes. For example, between the ages of zero and eighteen months, children are learning to trust that their basic needs will be met by a parent or caregiver. However, if a child's needs are not consistently and predictably met, they learn not to trust the intentions of their caregivers, which sets off the fear center in the brain (called the amygdala). Without intervention, this child may learn to be mistrustful of adults, be overly concerned about their own safety, and be fixated on meeting their own needs. This is a frustrating and confusing presentation for adults who are trying to convince a child that they are safe and cared for when the child's brain is keeping their body in a chronic state of hypervigilance.

One of the most fascinating aspects of our work as trauma therapists is putting on our detective hats and looking at current behavior to answer the question "What happened when this aspect of development should have been taking place?" When we don't have historical information to draw from, we can listen to and observe what the child's body is telling us through its current experiences. By taking what we have observed and pinning it on a timeline, we are able to narrow down when the child's development was interrupted.

> ### Using Timelines to Understand Complex Behaviors: Eleven-Year-Old Boy with Persistent Toileting Challenges
>
> **Step 1:** Begin by placing the challenging behavior or missed milestone on the timeline:
>
> In utero 0 1 2 3 4 5 6 7 8 9 10 (11) 12 13 14 15 16 17 18
> *Difficulty with toileting*
>
> **Step 2:** Identify the stage of development where this skill would optimally have been learned:
>
> In utero 0 1 (2 3) 4 5 6 7 8 9 10 11 12 13 14 15 16 17 18
>
> **Step 3:** Identify any life events or traumatic experiences that may have occurred at the same time:
>
> In utero 0 1 (2 3) 4 5 6 7 8 9 10 11 12 13 14 15 16 17 18
> - *Removal from biological parents' care*
> - *Inconsistent responses to toileting needs*
> - *Shame and consequences for toileting accidents*
> - *Increased fear responses in a new foster home*

Now that you have a visual representation of the behavior over time and within context, you may view it differently. You may also find yourself having a different emotional reaction to the behavior. Remember that what you *believe* about a behavior influences how you *feel* about it, which drives how you *respond* to it. When you take this eleven-year-old boy's whole life into consideration, it allows you to recognize that you might be trying to "fix" a challenging behavior that simply reflects a disrupted developmental milestone. The timeline clearly demonstrates what this child should have ideally learned between the ages of two and three, but this learning was delayed due to the complex trauma that occurred during and prior to that time. This is a fantastic reminder that parents need to meet their child where the trauma began instead of expecting them to respond like other children their age. It is an opportunity for parents to go back and give their child the experience they should have had at the time: a trusting, loving, safe caregiver to help them learn skills around toileting.

One way to understand the impact of trauma on functioning is to notice the types of fears, beliefs, and ideas a child is currently presenting with and match that with what we know about typical development. By "typical development," we are referring to children whose brains and bodies have not been significantly disrupted by trauma. When we observe traumatized children, it's as if their development was frozen in time and they are unable to move forward. A noticeable discrepancy exists between their chronological age (namely, how old they are based on their birth date) and their developmental age (namely, the age at which they function), which alerts us to consider what may have happened that delayed or skewed their development in this area. For example, a seventeen-year-old girl who is terrified of the dark and seeks to be close to her parents at night would alert us to a presenting behavior that does not match the expected response given the teen's age. The following table provides you with a quick reference guide on typical developmental fears. Use this as a reference point when you are unsure if the behavior you are seeing is developmentally appropriate or not.

Infancy **(0–18 months)**	• Stranger anxiety • Unexpected objects or people • Loud noises • Shadows • Separation from parents • Changes in routine • Fears related to toilet training
Early Childhood **(18 months–4 years)**	• Separation anxiety • Death or dead people • Ghosts or monsters • Insects • The dark • Storms • Costumed characters
Primary School **(5–10 years)**	• Natural disasters • Serious illness • Specific objects • Being harmed by bad people • Storms • Violence • Scary events they hear about in the media
Middle and **High School** **(11–18 years)**	• School performance • Future transitions • Peer rejection • Exclusion from events or activities • Gender differences • Exams

Knowing the impact of trauma at different developmental ages helps us ask the right questions so we can connect the current behavior or stalled area of development with early experiences. It can also help us predict what aspects of a child's functioning or behavior might be impacted in the future so we can proactively intervene. For example, seventh-grade students often have the opportunity to go on a three-night field trip away from home, which is a common rite of passage during this stage of development. If a child does not have the foundational attachment experiences necessary to manage this experience, we can help facilitate their exit from this activity without inducing shame or social repercussions, or we can make accommodations to allow the experience to be a success. For other kids who want to go on the trip but are afraid to do so, there may be a great internal struggle. They might take their anger out on their parents because they aren't able to manage this experience and are frustrated with feeling different from their peers. In this case, the parent and child will both benefit from planning ahead to either support the child through the experience or create an alternative option that will reduce the disappointment of not attending this one.

When Trauma Is Preverbal

Preverbal trauma is any traumatic experience that occurs before a child develops the ability to speak or communicate using verbal language. Since few of us really remember what happened to us before the age of two or three, people assume that those experiences do not impact the way we live. In fact, we've found that many parents mistakenly believe that since preverbal memories occur before the development of language, these memories are "out of sight, out of mind." While it is true that we don't hold our preverbal memories in the same way that we hold other memories, preverbal memories can nonetheless impact us profoundly. We just do not remember preverbal experiences in the same way that we might remember an incident that happened a week ago. For example, if we run into an old friend at the grocery store, we create a memory of this incident that is stored in the form of a story we can retrieve later. However, memories that happen before we have the capacity for language are stored in our senses, without words. This is significant because preverbal memories are imprinted on our sensory or emotional experiences, allowing them to become activated whenever we experience a similar feeling in the present. Over time and with gained insight, we can understand which sensations or emotional experiences are likely to cause a reaction.

For many parents, it is challenging to work with preverbal triggers because their child can't name these events or doesn't appear to have cognitive awareness of them. As a result, you might be wondering if your child has experienced more traumas than you are aware of. It's unlikely you can just ask them and get the information that way since preverbal memories do not require conscious awareness for them to be activated. In addition, if you have adopted or are parenting a child in government care, you may not have access to their history. Similarly, if your child moved between two different homes due to separation or divorce, you might not always be aware of their experiences. It is much more likely you will see evidence in the way they respond to sensory experiences, react to stressors in their environment, and engage in relationships.

The Moreno Family: Preverbal Trauma

The Moreno family recognized over time and through observed behavior that their daughter, Isabel, whom they had adopted two years ago, was hypervigilant even in their family home. Every time the doorbell rang, she had a big reaction. They would see a look of fear flash across her face and watch her little body search for the most creative hiding spot. It took much coaxing and reassurance to draw Isabel out from under furniture, inside cupboards, and behind the long, heavy living room curtains. This was confusing for her parents, and they felt frustrated that this was a continual problem they could not resolve despite their efforts to soothe, reason with, and reassure her.

Mr. and Mrs. Moreno decided to reach out for help from a trauma therapist and expressed curiosity about the relationship between Isabel's fear and her early history before she joined their family. They were curious about whether this was related to any of her early trauma history. After some discussion with the therapist about Isabel's early history, they started to piece together the connections. Isabel started off her life living with her biological mother in a house where people were constantly coming and going, drugs were being sold, and police raids were frequent. They presumed that the sound of the doorbell ringing created an increase in cortisol for both the biological mother and Isabel alike, which created a neurological association between doorbells and danger. The doorbell sound preceded many different types of danger, and the frequency with which this happened left them both in a constant state of hypervigilance. Without any direct intervention, this pattern had continued in the Moreno home for many years, leading to a well-established pattern of behavior.

When you read the Morenos' story, you may have had a particular behavior or pattern of responding come to mind that you've noticed in your child and found confusing. Perhaps this pattern of responding has continued even when it doesn't make sense in your child's current world. Use the timeline exercise you learned earlier in this chapter and put on your detective hat. (You can find a blank template of the timeline exercise in appendix A.) Take that behavior or pattern of responding and compare it to the timeline of your child's life to see if it might have made sense at any other point in time. This will help you to place these behaviors and responses in a context that does make sense.

It might feel a bit overwhelming to learn about all these different forms of trauma, and you might be wondering if you even understand all the ways your child's life experiences have impacted them. You also might be wondering if your child has experienced trauma even if they don't seem to be showing any signs or symptoms of trauma in their daily behavior right now. Certain behaviors that you may mistakenly ascribe to "willful defiance" or "ADHD" may actually be related to developmental trauma. Similarly, a child's trauma symptoms may only be activated during certain developmental periods but not steadily across childhood. Our goal thus far is to give you an understanding of the language of trauma and to increase your awareness of the many ways trauma can impact children. We believe this will make it easier to recognize the ways trauma has impacted *your* child. In this next section, we'll shift gears by providing a brief overview of how trauma therapy works for kids. While it's easy to feel hopeless when you consider the many ways that trauma can impact child development, know that there *is* hope for healing.

What Is Trauma Therapy?

If your child has attended more traditional talk therapy or play therapy, you may have noticed that while they may have made progress in some areas, they still struggle with frequent triggers—that is, reminders of the past trauma—that are easily activated and don't seem to resolve over time. These triggers can come in the form of sights, smells, sounds, thoughts, people, or locations that cause unexpected, and often intense, behavioral reactions. As a result, you may be pursuing trauma therapy because you recognize that previous interventions haven't been able to address the root cause of what keeps your child stuck in unhelpful patterns of behavior.

Trauma therapy is different from other types of therapy in that it is often less focused on addressing present issues and concerns. Instead, trauma therapy involves processing past memories and experiences, as well as providing clients with specific techniques to reduce the intensity of triggers that bother them to this day. For example, it may teach them how to go into a safe space in their mind to reduce the severity of dysregulation when they encounter an upsetting thought, feeling, or experience. Child-specific trauma therapy is even more specialized because it recognizes that when traumatic experiences happen during important developmental periods, those aspects of development are impacted.

Although the term *processing* is used often in the counseling world, the idea of it can feel a bit mysterious. You might be wondering what it means to process a memory or an experience given that certain memories can be stored without words. When we say "processing," we are referring to the process of accessing a memory that is held either in implicit memory or explicit memory. Implicit memories are subconscious memories that are stored in our senses, so we can't tell a story about them. We still *know* them, and they still impact us, but we can't share them with someone else with words. This is how preverbal memories are stored. Explicit memories, in contrast, can be consciously recalled via spoken words, so we can tell a story about what happened. For children and youth with developmental trauma, many of the memories that drive their behavior are implicit. In trauma therapy, we process both implicit and explicit memories.

You might be wondering how we can help a child process a memory that they can't talk about. Well, there are several different ways to do this, and the exact process will depend on the modality that your therapist uses, but it can involve connecting to the memory via play, art, body movements, bilateral stimulation, or conversation. During memory processing, the goal is not to erase the memory but to reduce or remove the emotional intensity attached to it so it no longer drives the child's thoughts, feelings, and behaviors. Different trauma therapies use different tools to facilitate memory processing, which you'll learn about in chapter 5.

Janice and Eric: Developmental Trauma and Missed Milestones

Janice came to counseling with her son, Eric, with the hope that he would be able to process the emotional and physical impacts of his developmental trauma. The biggest area of concern for Janice was the challenges Eric had with toileting. Eric was seventeen years old chronologically and about nine years old developmentally, yet his toileting was consistent with what we would expect of a toddler. She intuitively knew that Eric's challenges with toileting were related to his early trauma, but she didn't have the full story of what his life was like at that age. The family doctor had ruled out any physical explanation, and all typical efforts to improve this area of functioning had been unsuccessful so far. An occupational therapist had supported the family in understanding some of Eric's sensory issues and helped him become more connected to the physical sensations in his body, but despite all this time and effort, the struggles around toileting persisted.

Eric was unable to notice when he needed to use the bathroom, would make a big mess when he did use it, could not seem to remember to wash his hands or flush the toilet, and was typically resistant to offers of support. He could not engage in a logical conversation about what was happening to him, what he needed, or what felt good or not. Janice was hoping that by uncovering some of Eric's early traumatic experiences, they might find the answer to the persistent toileting concerns.

Her hunch about this was correct. Once she had helped Eric process his early experiences, his resistance to parental help decreased. This allowed Janice to walk Eric through the

> stages of toilet training in a way that felt good and safe for him. Within a few months, Eric was using the toilet in a way that was consistent with his developmental age and both parents and child were satisfied with this progress.

What Does Trauma Therapy Look Like?

There is a wide range of "normal" when it comes to how children and their parents engage in therapy. Some children show up with the mental space, energy, and support they need to delve deeply into their experiences and find relief. Others spend many years working through their trauma. The frequency of sessions can also be quite variable depending on where children are in the process, how urgent their presenting symptoms are, and the extent to which they are able to tolerate the intensity of trauma work. Some children may attend weekly, biweekly, or monthly sessions, and at times when they are processing big traumas, they may require two sessions a week for a short period of time.

The overall length of trauma therapy is also affected by several factors, including health benefits, therapeutic goals, and current life struggles. For example, some families arrive at therapy with a very specific concern they want to address, while others arrive with the more global goal of addressing developmental trauma. These are two vastly different goals that will result in a significantly different number of sessions. Similarly, a family's therapy goals may shift as different experiences start to surface for the child. It can be tricky when you have a particular expectation of how long therapy will last and you find yourself surprised by the depth of work that needs to be done to support your child.

In addition, some children may be in the middle of a very difficult time in their lives, and they'll need support to navigate those struggles before they are ready to move into processing work. This will naturally increase the number of sessions required to achieve their overall goals. Some children are also open to processing trauma that occurred during a particular developmental stage but are resistant to processing others. For example, a child may be open to processing an experience where they were bullied in grade school but unwilling to process an experience of sexual abuse as a preschooler. As a result, they might benefit from attending weekly or biweekly sessions for a period and then taking a long break until they are ready to tackle other traumas. Finally, when children are in government care and constantly moving from one home to another, they may not have the capacity to process their early attachment losses until they have arrived in a stable or permanent placement that allows them to begin experiencing secure attachment.

As you consider the frequency of sessions that is right for your family, know that the consistency of therapy can have a significant impact on your child's ability to heal. As you work to create consistency, it is important to consider when it makes sense to start trauma work, when it makes sense to take a break, and when a change in frequency is required. As you'll learn, there are many aspects of trauma therapy that can be very exhausting for anyone participating. While the actual activity happening in a session may seem simple, the reorganization happening in the brain and body is a demanding experience. Many children and parents will leave trauma therapy sessions feeling tired and unable to manage daily life tasks immediately following the experience. You'll learn more about what happens in trauma therapy in chapter 10.

CHAPTER 2

How We Provide Trauma Therapy to Children with Attachment Losses

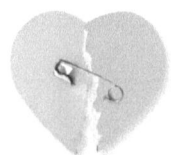

This chapter will take you on a journey that describes how we developed the ideas that shape this book. Our experience tells us that when you understand what is happening in therapy (and why), you are better able to stay connected with the process even when it gets hard. It also makes it easier to recognize the changes in yourself, your child, and your relationship. With this in mind, let us share how we got here.

Back in the early 2000s, our clinical work with children and youth looked much like it did with most therapists. We would talk with parents who brought their child to therapy, gather their concerns, and then have one-on-one sessions with the child. We would share progress with the parents and ask for feedback or answer questions outside of session time. As we began to see more and more children with attachment losses and trauma, we grew frustrated with the lack of sustainable progress after children left the emotional container of the therapy room. It became difficult to translate for parents what we were seeing in sessions and to engage them outside of sessions. Parents were essentially out of the loop, which left children with only one hour a week where someone understood the connection between their trauma and the daily behaviors their family was witnessing. We noticed that for youth who were floating through the foster care system, this lack of parental involvement had an even greater impact on their ability to heal from trauma, which further led us to advocate that every child come to therapy with a consistent adult who could support them throughout the process.

When there is no available adult, the therapist becomes the attachment figure, leaving the youth at risk of another sudden loss when therapy is discontinued due to factors outside the therapist's or youth's control (e.g., change in social worker, funding cuts, placement moves).

CJ: Therapy Without a Consistent Parental Figure

CJ was a middle schooler when she started sessions. She was referred to therapy after several recent episodes of rage threatened to end one more foster placement. She arrived at our office for the first time with her current foster parent. It was apparent from the first moment I laid eyes on her that she was anxious and seeking connection. Her body language was calling for her caregiver to pay attention and get close to her. Anyone who is familiar with typically developing adolescents—who often seek independence rather than closeness—might wonder what was happening with this child.

As CJ literally bounced into my office, the vibrating energy from her body felt as though chaos was orbiting around her. I would later discover this feeling was consistent with the way all the adults in her life described her. CJ had more foster placements than I could count after multiple reports of abuse by her biological parents landed her in care at the age of five.

My first goal for CJ was to help her stay in her current home. I requested the opportunity to focus my initial work on the parent-child relationship, but the changes couldn't come fast enough, and CJ was moved shortly after.

The new placement was a group home where there was no consistent parental figure that CJ could bring to counseling sessions. Thinking this was just a temporary placement, I agreed to see CJ alone until a suitable parental figure could be identified. It was remarkable to me that CJ was still looking for adult connection. She had been abandoned and disappointed so many times, yet her hope remained strong. Over the years, I watched as this hope and dream for a family of her own led her from placement to placement.

During this time, CJ started to use the sessions to work through the different developmental stages of attachment. She started by looking for nurturing, feeding, and soothing, as infants often do. She then moved to play and wanting to be seen, noticed, and celebrated, as toddlers and young children often do. She would get angry if I couldn't read her mind. She would only share with me and no one else. She wanted to be with me all the time. We worked through many different boundaries that were consistent with what would be developmentally appropriate for early school-age children to learn (for example, learning to understand what she could control and what I could control). Some of these skills became transferable to other adults who supported her, but her strong preference was to connect with me, as our connection allowed CJ to slowly redo what had gone so wrong for her over the years.

As no caregiver was ever identified for this young girl, she continued to be moved to different group homes based on what was available. It was during one of these moves that her case worker announced that her new group home had its own

> therapist, and the agency had a policy that this therapist work with all the children in their care. This sudden and unexpected move away from me—when I had played the role of a primary attachment figure—was so overwhelming that she refused to come back for a goodbye session. No follow-up information was ever provided, and I have no idea if CJ ever found a replacement attachment figure or what impact the loss had on her.

We had observed the limitations of processing developmental trauma for only one hour a week and wanted to do more. So, we decided to take a pause; review what we knew about child development, attachment, and complex trauma; and see where it led us. We started to explore the parent-child therapies that were currently available, which were primarily focused on supporting younger children through parent-child play therapy sessions. We worked to adapt this model for older children and teenagers so their needs could be met through play or shared attention on a common activity in the therapy space. We noticed that this had a profound impact on the parent's capacity to support their child at home and the degree of relational satisfaction being reported. This was amazing news!

Evan and Tracy: Prioritizing Parent Involvement in Session

Evan originally sought therapy for his daughter, Tracy, to help her work through a deep trauma history he knew was impacting her on implicit and explicit levels. He wanted Tracy to be able to work through the hurt so she could experience a life free from those burdens. Unfortunately, their first experience of counseling was not supportive of these goals and caused a bigger rupture in their relationship.

In particular, Tracy's therapist did not include Evan in treatment, only speaking to him at the end of each session to give a brief update or make a request on Tracy's behalf. This was causing tension in his relationship with Tracy, as he felt that Tracy was using her counseling time to create division between the two of them. The therapist didn't understand Evan's concerns and assured him that the approach she was taking was an appropriate therapeutic intervention for teens. It was devastating for Evan, who had spent so many years working to build a secure attachment with his daughter. After several months of therapy, Tracy's counselor moved to a different practice, and Evan was left to find a new counselor for Tracy.

Fortunately, Evan's experience in our office was the opposite of his previous experience. I met with him for multiple parent-consultation sessions, where we discussed Tracy's history (including her attachment traumas), explored challenging behaviors in the home, and reviewed strategies Evan could use that would support his attachment to his daughter. We also decided that due to Tracy's strong connection to her previous counselor, Tracy's initial sessions would be virtual, and they would include her dad. I made an intentional decision to set up the sessions in a way that would allow Tracy to see the difference between her previous counseling experience and her new counseling experience. I also prepared Evan for how hard this change would be for Tracy at first because it was not what she was used to.

During our first parent-child session, I made a conscious effort to prioritize Evan as the attachment figure and the person who knew Tracy best. As I continued to look to Evan, Tracy also began to turn to her dad. They still went through hard times where they disagreed with each other, but Tracy began to see Evan as someone who provided

> comfort and support, who made space for the hard things to be named, and who could bear witness to the difficult processing she was doing in sessions. Their relationship outside of sessions drastically improved too. By shifting to a different counselor with whom Evan and Tracy were both part of the therapy process, they could finally see growth in their relationship and in Tracy's healing journey.

Unfortunately, as we continued working with families, we noticed that some of the therapies we had been using did not seem to have the capacity to reach the deep wounds that many children were presenting with, particularly with regard to developmental trauma. The parent would make some initial gains in their capacity to be attuned to their child—and the child would show some improvement in their ability to regulate—but the triggers remained unresolved and continued to activate the child regularly. So, we began exploring some of the most powerful trauma therapy modalities available to us at the time, primarily eye movement and desensitization reprocessing (EMDR), Lifespan Integration (LI), and Observed Experiential Integration (OEI). These interventions offered us a new set of tools that effectively resolve traumatic experiences.

Throughout our training and early implementation, it became apparent that these modalities were most often used for children and adolescents in individual sessions that didn't include parents. There weren't any protocols for including parents in the therapy other than having them be present in the room to act as an emotional support. We wanted to do something different, but we knew it needed to be grounded in the science of child development rather than our intuition. To help you understand how we arrived at our conclusions about best practices, the remainder of this chapter walks you through some of this science.

The First Relationship Shapes the Brain

The relationship that an infant in utero has with its mother becomes the template for all future relationships. Throughout pregnancy, both baby and mother become familiar with each other's movements, sounds, and smells. The baby experiences the mother's heartbeat, becomes accustomed to the sound of the mother's voice, and, in times of stress, absorbs the mother's hormones. The mother can feel it when her baby is moving and may sense when her baby is calm and relaxed. She might experience her baby reacting to her voice and movements. This connection in utero is the beginning of what is meant to be a lifelong relationship. For the baby's developing brain and body, the expectation is that this relationship will always exist.

The rhythms of life also begin in utero as the baby's body and brain adapt to its environment. When a pregnancy is healthy and the mother is not stressed, the infant experiences a calm, safe, and comforting environment even before being born. However, if a mother experiences depression, prolonged stress, or a lack of safety that impacts her own physical and mental well-being, the developing baby feels the stress of the mother. When an infant is exposed to chronic stress or trauma in utero, these experiences can leave a lasting neurobiological impact on their body and brain. Without effective intervention, the way this infant responds to stress throughout childhood, adolescence, and adulthood can be traced back to these early experiences.

Babies are born ready to connect. If you watch a newborn in the hours just following delivery, you will see how the baby looks for their mother, settles with close contact, and seeks food and comfort from her. It's so incredible how at birth, an infant's auditory system is mature enough that it can turn toward the direction of the mother's voice. When a mother is physically and emotionally healthy, she responds to her baby's cues by watching, holding, talking to, rocking, and feeding her baby. Through these repetitive and predictable interactions, the baby feels calm and safe, which keeps their nervous system regulated.

Importantly, a mother's own attachment security impacts the way she responds to her infant, which then influences how secure the child's attachment is. The more attuned the mother is to the child's emotional and physical needs, the more synchronous the dance between them and the more secure the attachment becomes. If the mother can predict what the child needs to regulate their nervous system effectively, the infant will be left with the assumption that all caregivers will be like this. However, if the child's needs are not met appropriately and they are not reliably soothed when they are upset, then the child will learn not to rely on attachment figures. The infant internalizes these early experiences in their developing brain, which informs how they respond to any new relational experiences.

Early Experiences with Novelty and Familiarity Impact Attachment

Research into the neurobiology of attachment has found that the brain's reward system plays a key role in the formation of secure attachments in childhood (Chambers, 2017). A brain's reward system is essentially made up of two dichotomous systems: a novelty-seeking system and a familiarity system. Early in life, the novelty-seeking system is thought to be more active, seeing as the mother's face, smile, and body language are all novel, so the infant is drawn to explore it. However, as an infant interacts more with their mother, they start to experience comfort in the familiarity and no longer need the experience of novelty. In this way, familiarity becomes the infant's preference during this sensitive period of development. However, if the brain's reward system does not fully develop during this period due to interruptions by abuse, neglect, or a change in caregivers, then the child may continue to seek out novelty and prefer it over familiarity. It's easy to see how this can impact a child's ability to build secure relationships in the future.

Since children who have experienced multiple caregivers may never have had the opportunity to move from the novelty-seeking stage to the familiarity stage, it is one of the key developmental tasks they must accomplish once they are settled into a permanent family. It means that we must work with a child's reward system and essentially redo the experience of moving from novelty to familiarity and finding comfort and security in this. Imagine a baby staring up at a parent for hours a day while being held for feeding. They are constantly exploring with their eyes and eventually their hands. This experience can be repeated for older children by providing them with repeated opportunities to connect with their parent in a physical sense (allowing them to explore the parent's facial features, put their hands in the parent's mouth, and touch them constantly) and also by asking the parent questions. In the beginning stages, children need to experience repetitive and pleasurable experiences with their *parents*, so some families choose to limit the number of adults who meet the child's primary needs for feeding, toileting, reassurance, affection, and attention. Once the child develops a preference for their new parents, then other caring and trusted adults can become active in the child's world. The goal is to help children learn that preferred adults are more desirable than strangers.

Ben and Susie: Novelty Seeking

Susie had been adopted only a year before starting therapy. At her first therapy session, she bounded into the room without a backward glance toward her dad, Ben, who had brought her. After some discussion, I understood that this was Susie's reaction to any adult she believed was interested in spending time with her. New relationships were attractive to this child, and she was drawn to them, obviously preferring the company of a new adult over her parents. Her parents had noticed this behavior and assumed she had a healthy adjustment to adults and separation, but they did at times wonder if she should be developing a stronger preference for them. I reminded Ben of his role in the session and invited him in, explaining to Susie that he would be joining us. Susie appeared a bit disappointed and surprised.

In a separate parent-only session, I explained what was happening in Susie's body and why she was reacting the way she did toward adults. We explored different ways that Susie's parents could encourage her to prefer the primary adults who cared for her. I also explained that it was important for Susie to have pleasurable and exciting experiences *with her parents* so these novel experiences would happen together. They took this advice to heart and went to new places, tried new food, and had new experiences together while Susie explored her world within the safe container of her relationship with her parents. I also encouraged the parents to have conversations with other adults in Susie's life and explained that these other adults needed to refrain from offering these experiences to Susie until she had learned to look to her parents for them.

Throughout our work together, I discovered that Susie had a belief that "I feel safe if I'm making everyone happy and they like me." This is what had led to her preoccupation with creating an instant connection with any adult in her world who could potentially be a threat. However, as Susie began finding security in her primary attachment relationship, her parents noticed that this behavior diminished without them having to address it directly. She began to

> feel safe with the attention and protection provided by, and connection with, her parents, and she no longer felt the need to self-protect by drawing all adults close to her.

Secure the Base First

Think back to an experience of watching a toddler or young child playing with building blocks and getting frustrated when their tower repeatedly falls over. What they can't conceptualize at that age is that they need a sturdy foundation to hold the weight of the blocks to achieve their goal of getting the structure big and tall. An adult observing their efforts might intervene when the child is open to learning and teach them how to build their tower by creating a secure base. This solid foundation gives them the platform to make their big ideas happen.

The concept of attachment works in a similar way. Without the building blocks of attachment as their foundation, the skills we try to teach kids will result in a topple-over reaction. Secure attachment occurs when a child experiences a caregiver who consistently meets their needs in ways that are safe, nurturing, and responsive. It occurs when a parent is sensitive to their child's needs and seeks to reduce situations where the child may feel overwhelmed. The child learns that they can turn to their parent in times of distress and knows they will reliably receive a comforting response.

If a child has more than one attachment relationship, each relationship will differ based on the caregiver's ability to meet the child's needs, particularly when that child is physically hurt, ill, upset, or frightened. For example, the child may have one caregiver who responds in a loving and predictable way, but another caregiver who responds in a rejecting and unpredictable way. While this may be a confusing experience for a child, the mere presence of that one secure attachment figure will act as a protective factor in the child's long-term emotional and psychological health. This is key information to remember if you are co-parenting with someone who does not share the same values of attachment-based and trauma-informed parenting. Your caring and attuned presence can still make all the difference.

By providing this secure base for your child, you provide them with the two foundational experiences they need to feel capable of exploring their past trauma. The first is a feeling of being *known* and the second is the feeling of being *safe*. When a child feels safe and known, they can venture into the difficult feelings related to the traumatic experiences they have intentionally pushed away. Now the child can revisit painful memories and open old wounds that were stored away until they were safe enough to feel them again. Indeed, the most profound and foundational discovery we have made in our clinical work is that when a child can finally experience their first secure attachment relationship, it creates a pathway for them to move toward healing and growth. Given the profound impact that a secure attachment has on all areas of a child's development, it only makes sense that we would centralize this experience in the therapeutic process.

CHAPTER 3

When You Need to Do Your Own Work

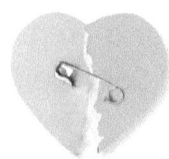

We imagine that reading and understanding more about childhood trauma may naturally lead you to reflect on what happened to *you* as a child. Maybe you have already participated in therapy extensively, or perhaps you have never considered it. It is natural for you to make connections between your own experiences as a child and what might be happening to your child. If you are worried that your own experiences might get in the way, know that what happened to you is exactly where you need to start. As Dan Siegel and Mary Hartzell (2003) say, "Making sense of our life enables us to understand and integrate our own childhood experiences, positive or negative, and to accept them as a part of our ongoing life story. We can't change what happened to us as children, but we can change the way we think about those events" (p. xvi). Regardless of how much you have considered or addressed your own experiences up until now, this chapter will allow you to understand how your own work impacts how you show up for your kid.

There are some good reasons to seek your own therapy before joining your child in this work. Parenting a child with a trauma history is not something that everyone can identify with, and sometimes you just need to be seen, heard, and understood. Your family and friends may care a great deal for you and still not understand the complexities of your experience. You might also feel uncomfortable or hesitant to be completely honest with those close to you about the ways you feel about your child. In case you've never heard this before, therapy does not need to be a trip to the emergency room; it can be a checkup to proactively care for yourself.

Regula and Her Children: Parent Counseling First

Regula came to therapy with the hope of getting support for her three children, who had all experienced significant trauma. In her first session, it was apparent that she was exhausted. She had been parenting her children for eight years and felt like she had no support. She couldn't talk to anyone about what her life was really like, and the few times she had tried, she was shut down quickly. After just one session, she noticed how much she still wanted to share with her therapist and was pleasantly surprised by the relief she felt in her body. She wanted to do more sessions but felt guilty about possibly using resources that could otherwise be focused on the needs of her children. After sharing this concern with her therapist, she felt supported in prioritizing herself first, allowing her to share her emotions, take time to reflect on her needs, and feel heard in a way she wasn't anywhere else in her life. She was able to see how meeting her own needs would put her in a better position to support her children.

It is our hope that what you learn in this chapter will help you determine whether doing your own counseling work is something that is necessary in order for you to provide the support your child needs for their own trauma therapy. What we have found is that when parents participate in their own therapy—especially in the same kind of trauma therapy their child will be engaging in—it allows them to feel more confident and comfortable with the process. It also creates so much more compassion for the hard work that is required.

Addressing Your Own Trauma

As adults, we all carry with us parts of ourselves that experienced hurt, pain, and disappointment. If you haven't been able to help all of these parts heal yet, they can show up and surprise you when you are least expecting them.

Christa and Amir: An Unexpected Trauma Trigger

Christa started therapy with her nine-year-old son, Amir, and was enthusiastic about being in the room and supporting him to resolve his trauma. She had not felt the need to do any of her own therapy, as she had experienced a supportive childhood and had seen therapists over the years who had helped her manage anxiety.

Before Christa adopted Amir, he had experienced parental loss and multiple subsequent foster placements. She also suspected that he had endured some abuse, but there was no documentation in his adoption paperwork to back this up. She assumed that therapy would help uncover the deeper reasons for his explosive behavior and the difficulties they were having with attachment. As Amir gained comfort and confidence in the therapy room, he began to express more of his hurt and anger.

During one of their sessions, Christa was observing the therapist's empathy for Amir's description of an incident of rage, when she suddenly felt a surge of anger that started from her feet and shot through her body. She later described it as feeling like a lightning bolt had hit her. Her face became hot and red, her body became rigid, and her fists were noticeably clenched. The therapist noticed her demeanor change and was struck by the way Christa seemed so small and scared in the room. There was no time for the therapist to react, as Christa threw her purse on the floor and yelled, "You only care about him!" She ran out of the room, leaving Amir and the therapist stunned.

The therapist's first response was to soothe and support Amir by quickly explaining that sometimes parents get big and unexpected feelings and that both he and his mom were safe. Shortly after, Christa returned to the room, sheepishly apologizing for her abrupt and shocking response. She was confused by her own behavior but recognized that something inside of her was triggered by the way the therapist was supporting Amir.

Christa and the therapist planned a parent session to address this. During that session, the therapist was able to help Christa uncover a younger part of herself that didn't feel seen or heard. This younger part brought to mind memories connected to another relationship in Christa's past where she had felt unheard and small. Her adult self was able to connect with this wounded younger part that needed to feel safe and validated. With this new understanding, Christa could see that her younger part needed to be calmed and soothed before sessions, and it reminded the therapist to care for this part as well. Even though this was a difficult experience for Christa,

> she found herself more confident in attending sessions and more aware of her own ability to support and validate Amir.

Christa and Amir's story is a helpful reminder that parents sometimes do not realize they have early childhood experiences that need to be addressed. It is possible that your recollection of your childhood or adolescence does not include traumatic experiences and that those events come to mind only when you feel similar emotions in your present-day life. These lived experiences may cause you to become activated in therapy if they have not been processed yet. The following are all examples of unprocessed life experiences that you may carry with you. Look at the list and make note of the ones you identify with. Although you may not identify with many items there, most of us have had an experience or two in our childhood of not being heard or seen. For example, a parent may have refused to listen to your side of the story when you were in conflict with an authority figure, or a trusted family member may have looked the other way and pretended not to notice your distress when you were harmed. Any of these experiences can leave lasting imprints on a child.

Potential Unprocessed Life Experiences

- → Physical, emotional, or sexual abuse
- → Sexual violence
- → Domestic violence
- → Chronic neglect
- → Feeling unseen or unheard
- → Unmet needs in childhood
- → Loss of a significant person

→ Infertility

→ Traumatic injury or health issues

If you identify with any of these experiences, perhaps you feel confident in the work you have done to heal yourself, or perhaps this discussion is leading you to believe that there is still work for you to do. Or perhaps you're not sure whether you have processed these memories enough to no longer feel triggered by them. This might be the case if you've done some talk therapy but haven't actually processed the memories enough to diffuse the sensations that are held in your body. Regardless of where you find yourself in this discussion, you *are* a good candidate to support your child in therapy. It's more of a matter of what might need to be done before you start that process.

In addition, if you do not have any memory of your childhood, this is a good indicator that individual therapy will be helpful for you. There are good reasons why memories are not accessible, and that would be worth exploring. For example, perhaps you have no recollection of anything that happened prior to the age of eight. No one has offered you any explanation that would point to any "big T" trauma, but you get a "sense" or "feeling" that something isn't quite right whenever you encounter particular sensory triggers. That's because when experiences are too big or too intense for the brain and body to tolerate, they are not stored in your narrative memory but remain in your senses. As a result, you are unable to describe the experiences that these memories are attached to. Your brain is doing a really good job of protecting you from the fear or pain attached to this unprocessed trauma. According to van der Kolk (2014), "As long as a memory is inaccessible, the mind is unable to change it. But as soon as the story starts being told, particularly if it is told repeatedly, it changes—the act of telling itself changes the tale. The mind cannot help but make meaning out of what it knows, and the meaning we make of our lives changes how and what we remember" (p. 193).

Vicarious Trauma and Compassion Fatigue

In chapter 1, we discussed the various types of trauma that an individual might experience, ranging from single-incident trauma and complex trauma to developmental trauma and preverbal trauma. These are all forms of *direct trauma* that an individual might experience firsthand. However, it is also possible to experience *vicarious trauma*, which is a form of indirect trauma that occurs when you witness or hear about the traumatic experiences of others. Parenting a child with trauma is a common form of vicarious trauma. After all, if you are caring for a child in this situation, you will inevitably witness the impact of your child's hurt and pain. Vicarious trauma can also result from the repeated disruptions that trauma causes your child in their daily life, whether it's how they respond to food, how their body reacts to sharp noises, or how they are sensitive to any inflection in your tone of voice. It is traumatic to see that your own child is so easily triggered and feels afraid in their own home, with people who are safe.

Alberto and Natalie: The Heartbreak of Vicarious Trauma

Alberto's daughter, Natalie, has horrific nightmares, and her shrill screams often wake him in the middle of the night. The same scenario plays out again and again. He rushes to her room to comfort and soothe her. The way she looks at him when he comes into her room nearly stops his heart. It's as though she sees him as dangerous, and his attempts to comfort her lead to her screaming "no" and "stay away from me." Even though Alberto understands that this is her body's response to past sexual abuse that happened at night, it doesn't stop it from hurting him. He feels helpless to protect and comfort Natalie from her worst experiences.

The heaviness of these repeated experiences has led to his own experience of trauma symptoms. He struggles to fall asleep at night, his heart races when he lies in bed, and when he does finally get to sleep, he is often awakened by a wide variety of other sounds that occur in his environment. He feels helpless, which often manifests as anger. This dynamic sometimes leaves Natalie feeling as though he is irritated with her, but she doesn't know why.

You may also experience vicarious trauma as a result of participating in your child's therapy. We have seen this many times in our work with parent-child dyads, which is why we aim to keep the parent (and the child) within their window of tolerance by monitoring the pace and intensity of the session. The term *window of tolerance* essentially refers to the optimal zone of arousal within which a person can operate. When someone is within their window of tolerance, they are not overwhelmed or flooded by their emotional experiences. They are able to tolerate the discomfort of trauma processing without escalating into a state of hyperarousal (anxiety, hypervigilance, tenseness, defensiveness) or collapsing into a state of hypoarousal (numbness, disconnectedness, shutdown, paralysis). In therapy, noticing the window of tolerance helps us to push a little, but not too much.

It is crucial to address vicarious trauma when it surfaces; left unchecked, it can lead you to develop *compassion fatigue*, in which you have trouble accessing your compassion for your child because you have given so much of yourself to care for them. It's your brain and body's way of trying to protect you against the feeling of overwhelm. In the foster and adoptive world, this is often referred to as *blocked care*, and it can lead parents to regret their decision to bring children with trauma into their family. These parents have been wounded by their caregiving experiences and need their own support before they can be emotionally available to participate in parent-child therapy.

If you are feeling burned out, it might sound so much more appealing to just drop your child off for an hour with a therapist and go get a coffee. We get it. However, this approach will only provide you with temporary relief; it is not a long-term solution that will allow your child to heal from their trauma. We suggest that you think of individual therapy as an opportunity to focus on yourself, get your needs met, and feel like yourself again before you take on something else that requires so much from you. You deserve to get help too. You deserve to live without trauma symptoms taking over the way you think and feel. Doing your own work will benefit not only you but also your child. They will feel the difference in having a parent who shows up authentically.

Doing Parent-Child Work at the Same Time as Individual Work

At this point, you might be wondering whether you can go ahead and start your own therapy while simultaneously beginning parent-child therapy. You might be worried that if you put off your child's therapy to focus on your own, you'll miss the window to get the right care. Or perhaps you've finally reached the top of the waitlist and don't want to pass up the chance to work with an experienced therapist. There are a few things you can consider to help you decide whether it is in your family's best interests to do your own inner work at the same time as parent-child therapy. If you have a good deal of awareness of your own body and the way you process your triggers—and you have the skills to regulate yourself when these triggers come up—you may be in a better position to do both at the same time.

Time is another important factor, so consider your schedule and capacity to meet the demands of daily life. Doing your own therapeutic work requires a time commitment, both within and outside of the session. You might only need a few weekly sessions to work through your earlier life experiences, or it may be a yearslong commitment, particularly if you have multiple triggers you want to address. Sometimes it's hard to know this ahead of time, so you can always get started with a therapist and have a conversation with them to decide what is practical for you. Given the demands of your family life, you may want to start with one trigger to reduce the intensity of the emotional experience, and then reevaluate whether you have the time to move on to the next trigger on your list. Just like kids, you may need to "test out" a therapist and the process of therapy to see how you feel about it.

Julie: Pacing Yourself in the Process

Julie reached out to a trauma therapist both to begin her own work and to participate in parent-child therapy at the same time. She felt like she had made some space in her life due to a recent layoff and was eager to get the process started for her child. After a parent intake session, Julie decided to work on a specific trigger from her childhood, as she was surprised how much emotion was still connected to it so many years later. In sessions, she was highly emotional and commented to the therapist, "I only cry when I'm in here." Once she left the therapy room, she would box up this experience, put it away, and go back to her demanding role as a parent of a child with trauma. She wished she could keep processing this trigger outside of the therapy room—knowing this would help speed up the process—but she didn't feel she was entitled to the space to work this out.

Julie's identity and temperament played a role in how she responded to the expectations that were placed on her throughout her life. She was viewed by others as the "strong one" and played the role of supportive parent well. Her therapist reassured her that everyone works through therapy at a different pace and that it was understandable she only felt comfortable opening up about this trigger in therapy—where she felt like she could be her authentic self. Instead of pressuring herself to "do" therapy in the way she thought she should, Julie adjusted her expectations about how long therapy would take. At the end of a session one day, Julie reflected on how her own experiences with individual therapy had helped her understand that she would need to follow the pace of her child's body when it came to processing trauma. Her original expectations of how it would work and how long it would take had been challenged by her own experiences.

In addition, you'll want to gauge the strength and availability of your support system, as this will impact the mental and physical energy you can devote to processing work. Do you have someone who can step in and support you with daily tasks that would otherwise take up all your time? If not (and your plate is already full), you may want to remove something to make room for counseling. It won't be easy to squeeze this into an already packed schedule. We highly recommend you think about how to set yourself and your child up for success by making sure you both have the time and space to genuinely show up and be available to engage. We discuss how to navigate these types of logistical barriers in chapter 11.

Jenny and Olivia: Stabilization During Parent Therapy

Jenny and Olivia are raising two children who have experienced significant trauma. They are a busy family juggling several appointments, as their kids have diverse interests. Their laundry room reflects the many sporting activities their kids take part in each week. Although they know that the behaviors they are seeing in their children—for example, explosive tantrums, refusal to take direction, difficulty falling asleep, excessive jealousy between siblings, and physical aggression—stem from their children's trauma history, they have delayed what they know is necessary: coming to therapy.

During the initial intake session, Jenny and Olivia share their own childhood stories, and it becomes apparent that Jenny experienced a similar upbringing to her children's, while Olivia was raised in a supportive and nurturing environment. Neither parent has extended family that live anywhere nearby, and they recently made a big move to a new community, so they have no one to support them with daily tasks.

Jenny and Olivia originally thought that therapy would focus on their children's needs, and they are surprised when the therapist suggests working with Jenny to address some of the triggers that she experiences daily. They ask the therapist if Jenny can do this work at the same time as the parent-child therapy, but after just one individual session, they decide that without any additional support, it is going to be too much. Jenny is experiencing sleep disruptions and mood fluctuations, and she needs a lot of emotional support from Olivia to complete daily tasks. She can't imagine having to balance parent-child therapy on top of what she is already doing and is

> grateful for the space to work through her own memories first. Fortunately, this intervention alone is enough to positively impact the family dynamic, as Jenny is learning new ways to respond to triggers that allow her children to regulate themselves more effectively.

Unexpected Ways That Big Feelings Come Up for Parents

As we've discussed, one reason that individual parent work is so important is that it prepares you for the difficult feelings you might encounter when your child is working through their memories. For example, let's say that your child has a history of being neglected by past caregivers, and they accuse you of abandoning them when they are upset. This accusation would understandably be distressing—it's hard to hear that your child continues to feel alone and left out. You might wonder, *What is the point of devoting all my time and energy to this child when I can't fill their cup enough for them to feel connected and cared for?* It is triggering to feel like you are not doing enough and then have to stay beside your child without reacting. When you spend time with your therapist planning how you will respond in these moments, it makes the process more predictable for you. When the process feels predictable, you are regulated and able to authentically show up for your child in their experience.

> **Common Parental Triggers in Session**
>
> → Your child brings up a memory or incident that they have not shared with you.
> → Your child shares a behavior you engage in that makes them feel scared or ashamed.
> → Your child responds in a way that is atypical for them (for example, by becoming aggressive or swearing).
> → Your child rejects your comfort in the session, in front of the therapist.
> → Your child denies that you support them at home.
> → Your child denies a behavior or incident that you witnessed.
> → Your child accuses you of something you did not do.
> → Your child remembers a harm done to them by someone else and accuses you of that harm.
> → Your child talks about something that happened in the past as though it is still happening years later.
> → Your child accuses you of doing something to them that someone else did.

By preparing for these moments and processing your own emotions ahead of time, you will have a better understanding of what's happening in session. It's not all bad news either. These experiences, although triggering, are often the most transformational moments in therapy. Your presence beside your child when they have big feelings—that is, when you are present and attuned without attributing their experiences to your own failures—is healing for them. This is one of the ways that you help fill your child's cup.

Chapter 3 | *When You Need to Do Your Own Work*

Remembering Your Experiences at Your Child's Age and Stage

At some point in therapy, you may find yourself identifying with a particular experience your child is having based on a similar experience you had at the same age or developmental stage. It could simply be the experience of being an eleven-year-old girl or, more specifically, the experience of being treated poorly by peers in middle school. If you find yourself connecting with a negative experience that you haven't yet processed, you may become triggered. For example, you might react unexpectedly, respond as though you are still in the past, or view the current situation through the eyes of your childhood self. These all reflect your body's way of remembering the experience.

Similarly, you may find that there is a disconnect between how you and your child respond to the same experience. For example, imagine that your child is starting kindergarten, and you are instantly drawn back to the memory of your first day of school. Your body is flooded with feelings of excitement and joy as you remember longing to join your older siblings, who went to school before you did. However, this experience might be in direct opposition to that of your child, who is experiencing anxiety and dread toward the inevitable separation that will occur. This disconnect can be tricky if you are not aware of what is happening. Similarly, if your experience of kindergarten was lonely or scary, your body might still harbor those feelings, and your child might be concerned about their own safety based on what they are picking up from you.

Finally, it is possible that as your child shares their own experiences, you unintentionally make it about *you* and your own unmet needs at that age or stage. For example, let's say your daughter is sharing in session about how she felt scared when she was on the playground and excluded from her peers' game. She is flooded with feelings of shame, loneliness, and anger because this experience reminds her body of earlier attachment losses. You, too, are drawn back to your own experience of being excluded as a child and reminded of how isolated you felt then. Your own parents were dismissive, and you often felt alone with your feelings. You instantly shift into action mode and start making plans for how you will advocate for your daughter at school and insist on the other kids being held accountable for their behavior. While the therapist was trying to make space to process your *child's* earlier feelings of shame and loss, you shifted the discussion to action planning. Although you were aware of your own unmet needs, it was tough to slow down and remember the bigger picture.

At the end of the day, even if you are attuned and aware, sitting in your child's trauma therapy session is going to activate you. The more you have diffused those triggers through your own work, the easier it will be for you to show up with an open presence and be able to manage your own emotions in the moment. As we move into a more specific discussion of your role in parent-child therapy, we invite you to continue reflecting on your own experiences and how they may play a role in the way you show up in session. If you've read this chapter and realized that you need to do some of your own work, you may feel like putting this book down. We encourage you to lean in to processing your own experiences while you continue reading. There is so much more ahead that will help you make sense of the interconnections between your experiences, your child's experiences, and the process of parent-child therapy.

CHAPTER 4

A Parent's Role in Trauma Therapy

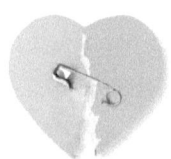

When seeking therapy for your child, you anticipate that your role will be to find a therapist, set up an appointment, and transport your child to and from each session. You are left hoping that the efforts you've made to find the right therapist, combined with whatever magical experiences happen during the counseling sessions, will make things better for your child. If you're lucky, you might even sneak in a quick shopping trip during the time your child is learning the strategies that will lead to significant life changes. Shopping for you and behavior change for your child—seems like a win-win! Of course, we are being a bit facetious, but on some level, this is appealing to busy, overwhelmed parents. However, given everything you've learned about trauma and attachment, removing yourself from the equation when you hold significant knowledge, insight, and love for your child seems counterintuitive, doesn't it? Indeed, what we know from years of clinical experience is that *you* are the missing piece in trauma therapy. Your involvement as the parent is transformational in helping your child heal.

Being involved in your child's therapeutic care may not seem like such a radical idea given that is what you do every day. You participate in other health care appointments and collaborate with other professionals to meet your child's needs. It only makes sense to do this with their mental health care as well. When you are there to witness your child as they process their hardest experiences, you show them that you see, hear, and understand their experiences. You show them that the thoughts and feelings they are expressing are not too much for you. There is no substitute for being in the room during those moments. By being present, your child does not need to explain to you afterward what happened in session because you will have seen firsthand the deep places they visited, the relief they felt, and the new insights they gained. Trauma leaves kids feeling alone in the world, even when they have a loving family, and when you can stay in the room and bear witness to their deepest hurts, they no longer feel alone in all of it.

Bessel van der Kolk (2014) perhaps put it best when he explained what an individual needs to safely engage in trauma therapy: "You have to find someone you can trust enough to accompany you, someone who can safely hold your feelings and help you listen to the painful messages from your emotional brain. You need a guide who is not afraid of your terror and who can contain your darkest rage, someone who can safeguard the wholeness of you while you explore the fragmented experiences that you had to keep secret from yourself for so long" (p. 213). We believe no one is better suited for this role than *you*.

Profound Insights from Observing and Participating

Immense therapeutic value comes not only from participating in your child's therapy but also from observing the therapist's interactions with your child. Many parents have told us that when they are able to watch the way we speak with and respond to their child, they get new perspectives on their child's day-to-day functioning, gain insights into the challenges their child is facing, feel empathy for how their child is impacted by their own behaviors, and learn ways to more effectively communicate about hard topics.

At the end of the day, sitting with and observing your child interacting with someone else gives you an opportunity to be one step removed from the conversation and notice your child differently. When the therapist expresses interest in a particular aspect of your child's life—one that you have heard way too much about already—you will notice what it feels like for your child to have someone express interest in their hobbies, thoughts, and ideas. You'll notice how your child speaks to and responds to the therapist in turn, which tells you what it feels like for them to be spoken to that way. Notice how this feels for you as well. Does it make you feel resentful or inspired?

Jane and Troy: Parent Participation Leads to Significant Insights

Troy was a twelve-year-old boy who joined his family through adoption six years ago. He had a significant trauma history, as he experienced a traumatic removal from his biological family at age two and then was in multiple foster homes after that. At home, Troy struggled with intermittent rage, which his mother, Jane, felt was a disproportionate reaction to minor issues with no obvious triggers. Jane finally decided to participate in parent-child trauma therapy after having gone through multiple unsuccessful attempts to take Troy to individual therapy.

Jane started the first session off by describing how the last week had been hard for the family. She described a specific incident when she asked Troy to move to a different room in the house for an hour because his presence was distracting his sibling from completing an important homework assignment.

Jane said she approached Troy gently, without urgency or correction, and explained why she needed him to move. Troy's response was instantly reactive in a way that seemed, from his mom's perspective, extreme given the circumstances. He started screaming, calling her horrible names, throwing whatever was within his grasp, and slamming doors as he moved from room to room throughout the house. He yelled repeatedly, "Why do I have to go?!" Jane walked away in exasperation, as after many similar experiences, she had come to feel that no matter how she approached a simple request, she could never predict how he would respond.

While Mom explained what had happened, Troy sat quietly, looking down at his feet. I wondered if Troy felt a sense of shame when he heard the story of his behavior, unable to make sense of it for himself. I asked him to think about what had happened and describe it in his own words. He said, "Mom made me move to a different room when I didn't want to. She doesn't care about how I feel. I don't know why I had to move in the first place."

I told Troy and his mom that I was going to repeat Troy's description of what it was like for him but remove just a few of the words. I explained that this strategy would help them understand what was so hard for him about this experience: "I had to move. I didn't want to. She doesn't care how I feel. I don't know why." I watched as Mom and Troy processed my words, noticing their individual reactions. I then asked Troy if there were other times in his life when he had experienced those same feelings. When he realized the connection between his current feelings of rage and the unfair and unsafe circumstances that had resulted in many previous moves, his eyes widened as he said, "Every time I had to move homes." Jane witnessed his experience, saw his facial expression, and clearly understood what the trigger had been. Her face softened and she moved closer to Troy. She and I both felt deep relief in Troy's next statement: "I guess I'm not just a horrible kid who rages at his mom for no reason."

A week later, Jane participated in a parent session with me where she reflected on the impact that this experience had on her parenting. She reported finding herself less reactive and more empathic whenever she saw big feelings from Troy. She was now able to see that his seemingly disproportionate reactions came from an earlier experience of pain. She could also see that those memories were often activated in the present without his conscious awareness. Jane felt prepared to step into these opportunities, knowing they were a chance for Troy to receive a different response from her and to find healing in the present.

As an active participant in trauma therapy, Troy's mom did not need anyone to work with her on building more empathy for her child. She also didn't need assistance in understanding the powerful impact that Troy's past continued to have on his current experiences. She was there to experience the moment, and it inspired a shift in her parenting response outside of the therapy room. This was an incredibly empowering moment for her as a parent, and it also served to strengthen their parent-child relationship in wonderful ways.

After reading Troy's story, you may be wondering, *Would I have been able to make those connections in a session with my child?* Or you may be wondering whether your child would be able to articulate themselves as well as Troy was able to. This example is meant to show you the power of being present in session—of sharing big moments and building connections.

Regardless of how much insight you can take away from the sessions, what you witness is a starting point to increase your knowledge and understanding of what is painful and challenging for your child.

You Are the Expert on Your Child

Your active participation in therapy establishes your role as the expert on your child. This is so important, as it reinforces to your child that you deeply know them. When the child sees the therapist as the expert, it can negatively impact their growing trust in you. We want your child to know that *you* are the person they can turn to when they have a need. You are the person who best understands their unique life experiences, triggers, and strategies for calming their body. Your child needs you as an advocate—someone who knows them so well and can predict what will set them up for success in each environment or relationship. They need protection when things feel "too much" so that the hard work they are doing in therapy is not undone.

We are asking your child to step into hard places, and we need you to honor the work they are doing by providing a soft place for them to land as they are healing. Your direct involvement allows you to know when they need extra one-on-one time, fewer demands or expectations than usual, or more emotional support to help them return to baseline. When we say "baseline," we are talking about how your child typically functions without any unusual stressors. This includes how much they typically sleep or eat, their toileting habits, their mood, their social interactions, and their family relationships. Another aspect of your child's baseline is their heart rate and body temperature. We are not suggesting that you need to monitor this closely, but making a note of whether your child runs hot when distressed or whether you can feel their heart beating faster than typical will alert you to their internal distress. By participating in your child's therapy, you can better understand your child's needs and advocate for them in all areas of their life.

Jason and Sergey: Discovering the Root of a Challenging Behavior

Jason arrived at the therapy office in search of some help for his son, Sergey, who had joined the family at the age of three. Sergey spent his first few years of life in a Romanian orphanage. Jason suspected that his son had experienced times as an infant and toddler when he did not have enough food to eat. He also wondered if the giving and taking away of food was used as a reward or punishment. He was currently concerned that Sergey's overeating and subsequent weight gain were contributing to his son's lack of interest in social engagement. Jason, an athlete, believed that eating was one of the most important ways to care for your body, but he was anxious about addressing his son's weight or eating habits, as he did not want to shame him or aggravate the problem. He was keenly aware that if his son's current eating patterns continued, there could be repercussions for his health. He also feared that Sergey would not have normal social experiences due to his excessive weight gain.

Things came to a critical point after a grocery shopping trip went terribly wrong. The result was a confrontation that involved yelling, throwing, and the eventual abandonment of the grocery cart as both father and son left the store very upset. Sergey felt that Jason was unfair and didn't care about the kinds of food he wanted. Jason reported that he had agreed to a few things Sergey wanted but said no to other items. Sergey was adamant that his dad refused to buy him anything he asked for. Jason was confused by Sergey's perspective, as he recalled offering choices and providing guidance on a balanced diet that was consistent with the conversations they'd had just prior to arriving at the store together. In fact, Jason reported that he was conscious of giving Sergey more yeses than noes and being reasonable in his limits.

With some reflection, both Jason and Sergey could see how hearing the word *no* when it came to food triggered the same feelings Sergey had when orphanage caregivers punished him by refusing to give him food. By sharing this story in session, Sergey's food-related triggers could now be discussed in the open, when it had previously been off limits. Taking the focus off Sergey's negative behavior allowed for curiosity about what triggered Sergey's reaction in the first place. Once Jason understood Sergey's trigger, he was able to see how important it was to protect his son from stressful food-related incidents while we worked to process his early experiences in therapy. Without Jason's direct involvement in therapy, he would have missed how Sergey's early experiences informed his current behavior. With this new understanding, they both agreed that Jason would grocery shop on his own for a while and increase choices at mealtimes to help decrease Sergey's dysregulation related to food, in both frequency and intensity.

As Jason and Sergey's story illustrates, when you witness the emotional impact of a particular event or experience on your child, you feel a sense of urgency to support them. Your natural inclination to protect your child gets activated, and it becomes your top priority. By participating in therapy, Jason was better positioned to advocate for his son's needs outside of the home. For example, he alerted Sergey's teacher that his son may need extra time to finish his food. He also asked the school to reach out to him immediately if they observed that Sergey needed more food on a given day. Jason was also sensitive to mealtimes and snacks when Sergey was in the care of a different adult. All of this was possible because Jason was able to see, feel, and understand what Sergey's behaviors were telling him, and he felt confident in how to respond.

Advocacy is not an easy endeavor. It can be incredibly exhausting and frustrating when other adults in your child's world don't understand what your child needs to feel safe. This is especially the case when you have a deep sense of knowing that something is harmful to your child, but you don't have the words to explain it. Witnessing how your therapist responds to your child in session is one way to learn how to speak to the other adults or professionals in your child's life. By hearing the language your therapist uses to acknowledge what is going on for your child, you can find the words you need to address other adults who would benefit from understanding your child's needs.

Challenges of Parental Involvement

Some children and teens are adamant that they don't want their parents to be a part of the counseling process. They may want the therapist's individual attention or believe they can't be honest about a problem without upsetting their parents or facing consequences for their behaviors. These fears are real even when they are unfounded. If you are a parent who has used a rewards-and-consequences model for managing your child's behavior, your kid might struggle more with this, as this model reinforces behavior in black-and-white terms (as "good" or "bad" behavior). In turn, your child may worry that the therapist will reject them or perceive them in a negative light based on your reports of "bad" behaviors. We've discovered that a rewards-and-consequences model does not work well for most children, and it is especially problematic for children who have an overactive stress-response system as the result of early trauma. For these children, the fear of punishment or loss of rewards activates the fight, flight, freeze, or fawn response, leading to behaviors that kids don't have control over.

> ### Fight, Flight, Freeze, or Fawn
>
> → **Fight:** The child becomes aggressive easily, destroys things, throws tantrums, or exhibits highly reactive anger that may be directed either outwardly toward others or inwardly toward themselves.
>
> → **Flight:** The child tries to escape stressful situations, is often anxious, avoids conflict by immersing themselves in activities, is chronically busy, or needs to be perfect.
>
> → **Freeze:** The child seems unable to make decisions, often spaces out, tends to be alone, often appears lazy, or may be verbally unresponsive.
>
> → **Fawn:** The child accommodates others at the expense of themself, engages in people-pleasing behaviors, is apologetic, has low self-esteem, feels taken advantage of, or complies to protect themself.

If your child is struggling with the idea of you attending therapy with them, try demonstrating to them that you can accept their big thoughts and feelings on a sensitive topic without overreacting or handing out consequences. By demonstrating that you can tolerate these situations without reacting negatively, you build trust and can potentially convince them that you are strong enough to handle their "big stuff" in session. We also recommend that you avoid promising rewards or prizes for attending counseling. It is, however, appropriate to pair counseling with special one-on-one meals, rituals, or soothing experiences. We will discuss the practical ways you can use rituals, routines, and experiences to support therapy in chapter 13.

In addition, your therapist can help your child feel comfortable with having you in session by modeling what each person's role will be. While the child's role is to share their story, your role is to help them feel safe, supported, and (most importantly) not alone in remembering these hard experiences. One way we model the role of the parent is to have an opening ritual where each person shares "something good" and "something hard." This exercise is a warm-up through which parents can practice listening to their child's experience and vice versa—whether or not they share the same perspective. It is also an opportunity for the parent to observe how the therapist empathizes with whatever the child's "something hard" might be. The therapist might also model the role of a parent by asking the parent to offer something that the child needs. This is a reminder that although the therapist may be attuned to what the child is experiencing, it is the parent's *response* to their child's experience that builds attachment security.

There are exceptional circumstances when it is not in your child's best interest for you to be involved in sessions, either at the beginning of trauma therapy or at all. These circumstances are rare and typically only happen when parents have intentionally or unintentionally behaved in ways that are abusive. For example, a parent may have frequently spanked their child as a method of discipline or a reaction to unwanted behavior, or they may have left their child in the care of someone who, unbeknownst to the parent, harmed the child. If a child or youth believes that you pose a significant threat to their physical or psychological safety (either currently or in the past), they will not be able to reach the place of safety in session that is required to process trauma. We need emotional connection in the therapy room to anchor the child in safety, and any perceived threat of harm leads to mistrust and, ultimately, emotional disconnection.

Children look to their parents—by analyzing their body language and facial cues—to assure themselves that they are good and safe. Emotional disconnection interrupts this natural process. When a parent is unable to offer this sense of safety in therapy, either because they don't know how or because they have become disconnected from their child, sessions become another experience where the child's feelings, needs, and fears go unacknowledged. This can occur when a parent (1) misses their child's cues for comfort, (2) dissociates when the emotional content reaches a certain level, (3) is dismissive of a particular emotional experience, or (4) frequently shifts the conversation to focus on themself instead of their child. If this is your experience, it is so important for you to stay involved, even if you are not attending parent-child sessions. Your therapist will need to step in and work with each of you individually until it is emotionally safe to have sessions together. Your therapist's job is to walk the line of assuring you that they have your child's best interests at heart while still challenging you to see your own blind spots.

If you find yourself struggling to view your child (and the problems they face) in a different light so you can be the empathic responder, the following chapters will offer additional insights and strategies to help you. You will come to understand more about how parent-child trauma therapy works and learn everything you need to set yourself and your child up for a successful therapeutic experience.

CHAPTER 5

Choosing the Best Therapist for Your Child

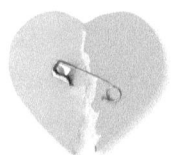

Finding the right professional for your family can be a difficult undertaking. If you've already done a Google search of trauma therapists in your area, you may have found either an overwhelming number of options or a rather sparse assortment from which to choose. In either case, you'll need guidance on where to start and how to make a good decision, as starting with the right therapist will save you so much energy in the long run. You know your child best, so some considerations you'll want to keep in mind when choosing a therapist include your child's preferences, tolerances, and individual needs when it comes to safety and comfort. We will walk you through these decisions in this chapter. We will also break down the different treatment modalities that therapists offer so you can feel more comfortable making an informed decision.

Finding a Trauma-Informed Therapist

The first place to narrow down your search is by looking for a professional who clearly states they work with children and youth, and the ideal choice will indicate that they include parents in therapy sessions. Reading a therapist's biography, alongside their website and social media pages, will often give you good information about what they believe, how they work, and what modalities they are trained in. We recommend looking for therapists who are trained in modalities such as EMDR, brainspotting, Theraplay, or LI (many of which we'll touch on in the following section), which are best suited for working with developmental trauma. In addition, make sure the therapist has the appropriate qualifications and credentials—such as a psychologist, social worker, marriage and family therapist, or mental health counselor—and don't get too caught up in whether they have "certifications" in any particular areas. Certifications simply involve taking an online course, which is very different from undergoing years of rigorous therapy training. We also suggest connecting with other parents who are struggling with the same issues to see if they have any therapists they recommend.

Once you have a few therapists you want to explore more in depth, you can contact their office, send them an email, or check to see if they offer an introductory call. Ask them questions like "What is your approach to helping parents understand and respond to rude, aggressive, and defiant behaviors?" "How do you help children with trauma make sense of their own behavior?" "How do you involve parents in therapy?" and "What would you prioritize when you start working with a child who has experienced developmental trauma?" These questions will help you understand how *trauma informed* they are. Therapists who are trauma informed prioritize a child's safety above all else, which means they are consistent, predictable, and empathic. If your child has big behaviors in the counseling office, you can see the difference in the way a trauma-informed therapist responds to those behaviors. For example, if your child is trying to hide a therapy toy to take home with them, a trauma-informed therapist will know your child is not "stealing" and will be able to place that behavior in the unique context of the child's experience. They might say something like "I know you felt good in here today and you want to take that good feeling home with you. You think that if you take that car and play with it at home, you might get the same feeling."

A trauma-informed therapist will also react with attention and care if your child swears or speaks disrespectfully to them in session. They will not deliver consequences, send your child away, or expect an apology. Instead, they might say, "I think that what I asked you gave you a terrible feeling inside and you are upset with me for making that happen." We can't emphasize enough how authoritarian and behavioral approaches are not safe or effective. Any suggestion that your child just needs a firm hand or that their behavior is willful and intentional should put up a red flag for you. A trauma-informed therapist understands that consequences, sticker charts, and obedience aren't the pathways to healing.

Choose a therapist who has the flexibility to meet you where you are—rather than being stuck in a particular methodology or intervention—which will allow your child to move into the trauma work at a pace that feels safe and tolerable. We strongly believe that while therapy is steeped in science, the practice of it is also an art. In the beginning stages, you may need some support to help your child develop a sense of safety and security in even attending sessions. For younger children, this can be done through play, and for older children, it can be done by taking the time to know them, learning about their interests, understanding their safety cues, and building their regulation skills. Finding a trauma therapist who can offer both safety and stability means that you are in the right place.

Consider Different Specialties and Modalities

There is a wide range of therapy modalities available for the treatment of trauma, some of which may be a better fit for you and your child. The fact that different therapies exist doesn't make one better than the other. It all depends on where your child is at and what your goals for therapy are. In addition, trauma therapists will often combine different modalities to meet the needs of their clients. For example, somatic approaches are almost always part of therapy sessions. Your therapist is constantly watching your child's body to notice what calms it, agitates it, and so on. For many children, having access to toys in session can be supportive as well, as it allows them to express their feelings without having to communicate with words. Therefore, some therapists utilize play therapy, sand tray therapy, and other forms of art therapy alongside trauma therapy, as this may be the best combination for some children.

In the following section, we've provided a few descriptions of the main trauma therapies out there. These descriptions are not meant to replace conversations with a therapist but, rather, to help inform you as you choose what might be the best fit for you and your child. It is also important to note that even though these therapies are taught with specific steps, protocols, and stages, each therapist is unique, and that will impact how they structure their session and how they implement the therapeutic modality.

Observed Experiential Integration

OEI is a trauma-processing therapy that targets the part of the trauma that is stored in the visual senses. OEI uses the visual pathways to support both sides of the brain in working together in a way that reduces anxiety and trauma symptoms. A client may be asked to talk or think about a challenging situation while covering their right eye and then switch to covering their left eye. This allows them to process the event from both sides of their brain.

The client may also stand on a balance board to help engage both sides of their brain as they follow the therapist's finger with their eyes, which is moving in the visual field to locate where the trauma is held. This allows the client to access the trauma through their vision without needing to talk about the trauma itself. This is a very freeing experience for many people who do not want to feel flooded by revisiting their trauma memories. OEI is a powerful set of procedures that can be integrated with other therapies, including Gestalt therapy, cognitive therapy, play therapy, and art therapy.

Brainspotting

Brainspotting uses spots in a person's visual field to help them process trauma (Grand, 2013). It accesses trauma trapped in the subcortical brain, which is the area of the brain responsible for motion, consciousness, emotions, and learning. Brainspotting is based on the theory that feelings from trauma can become stuck in the body, leading to both physical and mental difficulties. It is believed that brainspotting "resets" the brain's memory of a particular trauma or incident so that the emotional response experienced in the body and brain is no longer disturbing.

The session begins with a calming and regulating activity. The client is then asked to name a place in their body where they feel the most discomfort or distress and rate it on a scale from 1 to 10. The therapist then helps the client find their "brain spot"—the place where their eyes naturally focus when the physical discomfort is strongest. The therapist uses a pointer rod or their own finger to direct the client's focus to this spot, and they help the client locate the spot where they are becoming "stuck." As the client focuses on this area, they identify the feelings they are experiencing and then take some time to process the whole experience and what it may mean. At the end of the session, the client again rates their level of distress, which is typically lower than when they started. A benefit of using brainspotting with children is that they don't have to talk about their trauma or the memories that are coming up. They only need to talk about the sensations they are feeling and be able to rate their intensity.

Lifespan Integration

LI is a gentle, body-based technique that utilizes visual timelines to increase neural integration and heal trauma (Pace, 2015). LI relies on the body and mind's innate ability to heal itself. During LI, the client listens as the therapist reads a chronological timeline of memories from their life. These timelines help other memories surface spontaneously, with each memory being related to the emotional theme or issue being targeted. Some children can name their traumas and express what is coming up for them as they listen to the therapist read their memories. Other children are activated just by listening to their memories even though they are not able to say what is happening to them with words. Regardless, the process helps clients understand that they have survived the past and are living in the present.

Trauma-Focused Cognitive Behavioral Therapy

Trauma-focused cognitive behavioral therapy (TF-CBT) is a short-term intervention for children and adolescents who have experienced or witnessed a traumatic event. While traditional CBT treats mental health conditions such as depression and anxiety, TF-CBT focuses specifically on providing relief from the impact of traumatic incidents. It helps children identify the upsetting and inaccurate beliefs that cause them distress and teaches them skills to cope with the stressors of everyday life. Parents are involved in this intervention (nonoffending parents only) with a focus on providing them with psychoeducation on the impact of the trauma and teaching them parenting skills to address behavioral difficulties. There are three phases of TF-CBT—(1) stabilization, (2) trauma narration and processing, and (3) integration and consolidation—with parents engaging in joint sessions during the last few stages.

Eye Movement Desensitization and Reprocessing

EMDR is a structured therapy that helps the brain process and release the emotional distress associated with trauma (Shapiro, 2018). During EMDR, the client focuses on a specific trauma memory while simultaneously engaging in some form of bilateral stimulation. There are many types of bilateral stimulation available (for example, eye movements, sounds, and tapping), and the specific method used depends on the client's preference. As bilateral stimulation works to move the memory through different parts of the brain, the client is invited to share the thoughts, feelings, and sensory experiences they are having. Throughout this process, the client is instructed to rate the intensity of the memory, and they continue reprocessing work until the rating decreases in intensity.

Internal Family Systems

Internal family systems (IFS) is a transformative therapy that posits we are all made up of several subpersonalities, or parts (Schwartz, 2021). Just like members of a family, these parts can be forced into extreme roles that cause conflict within the system. IFS also postulates that we all have a core seat of consciousness within us known as "the Self," which can never be damaged. In IFS, clients learn how to access the Self so they can heal the various wounded parts they hold within themselves. IFS is a client-centered model of therapy, which means that the therapist follows the client's lead as they get curious about their parts, engaging with parts as they appear. With children, IFS is often combined with play therapy, where the child will direct the play, given the premise that the child's parts will come forward when the child feels safe and secure.

Challenges with Specific Trauma Interventions

When you are considering what type of therapy modality is best for your child, remember that you will want to take their individual needs and preferences into account. For example, LI involves a lot of verbal repetition of a child's story. Some kids can get really irritated with verbal repetition, so they might benefit from a therapist who can incorporate other somatic or expressive interventions to balance out that repetition. For example, children may draw an image they see in their mind when they think of a scary experience, repeatedly drum a particular pattern while processing a traumatic memory, or push against a wall as a way to demonstrate their own power in a way they couldn't in the past. Similarly, kids with visual difficulties might find it uncomfortable or impossible to follow a therapist's finger back and forth in EMDR. The alternative could be to use a set of tappers or buzzers, which would be a welcome alternative for some children but a sensory overload for others. In addition, some kids dissociate so automatically and so frequently that the therapist will need to engage their body regardless of what intervention is being used. We have found that incorporating a balance board into our work with children who dissociate allows them to naturally and comfortably stay present.

If you do not have a sense of how your child responds to fear, it's important that you start taking notice, asking questions, and getting curious. Trauma therapy can often feel like an attack on their system because they are being asked to recall horrific experiences—experiences that their brain and body have been protecting them from for a long time. To support your child in this process, you need to meet them where they are so you don't overwhelm their system. Have a conversation with your child's therapist as they develop a treatment plan that meets your child's needs, as you are in the best position to give the therapist the information they need to guide the intervention process and accommodate your child's unique physiology.

Lynn and Brodie: Finding the Right Intervention

Brodie had been coming to therapy with his parents for six months. However, Brodie's mother, Lynn, had a gut feeling that her son was not connecting well with LI, which was the therapy model being used. She knew that her son dissociated in intense ways when he was experiencing even mild distress, and she couldn't help but feel that her child was checking out during the listening part of the therapy.

In consultation with the therapist, they decided to add a balance board to sessions, and they noticed an immediate shift in how Brodie responded. Unlike previous sessions, where Brodie was often unable to hear what the therapist was saying when he started to feel overwhelmed, as soon as he got on the balance board, he said, "I can hear you now!" This also provided an opportunity to reevaluate the benefit of the current therapy model, given Brodie's propensity to shut down and dissociate in the face of stress or fear. He was given other options and chose to try brainspotting, which didn't require him to speak unless he wanted to. After switching to this therapy, Brodie's buy-in was far greater. He was then able to make more significant connections to his daily life and recognize the shifts in his trauma triggers.

Appointment Scheduling Matters

Over the years, we have found that when families maintain a consistent appointment schedule, it helps them get into the routine of therapy. However, you will need to find a therapist whose availability matches your schedule. Some therapists are only available during daytime hours, others have after-school or evening appointments, and some work on weekends. While you might prefer sessions that fall outside of school hours, this may be something you want to reconsider, especially if you have other children who might have other after-school obligations that require your attention.

If you find a therapist who is available on weekends or evenings, think ahead about any childcare you may need. If you have to cancel sessions frequently because you can't find childcare, this will lead to inconsistent attendance. In addition, holidays, extracurricular activities, and special celebrations often happen on evenings and weekends, so plan a time that won't create conflicts with other commitments on your schedule. Remember, consistency and predictability really help to regulate a stressed nervous system.

Consider, too, where your other child(ren) will be during session times, including who will be with them and what they will be doing. If your babysitter is going to take your child's siblings to the waterpark while your child attends counseling with you, this is going to create some jealousy and, potentially, conflict. (And, yes, this happens all the time!) Parents don't do this intentionally, but it nonetheless works against your child's ability to focus on counseling. They will likely feel that they are being punished for their behavior or that there is something "wrong" with them. They will also be distracted and anxious about the fun they are missing out on.

You also want to make sure there is a good match between the therapist's availability and your readiness to start the therapeutic process.

Chapter 5 | *Choosing the Best Therapist for Your Child*

It can be hard to keep a child engaged and ready to start therapy if you are on an eight-month waitlist. We have kept this type of waitlist at our practice, and we acutely feel the stress of parents who are ready to get started but don't have anyone available to see them. Finding a balance between waiting for the "right" therapist and getting started when the time is right for you and your child can be difficult.

Finally, we want to remind you that overloading a child with multiple new experiences at the same time can increase dysregulation. For example, starting school and starting therapy in the same week would be overwhelming for many children. If this is when a therapist becomes available, and you don't want to lose your opportunity to start with someone, consider having some parent-only sessions until your child has had an opportunity to adjust to these other life changes.

Ryan and Tia: Timing Matters

Ryan was elated when he received a phone call letting him know that there was space for his daughter, Tia, at the counseling agency, which he had been waiting eight months to get into. As he looked at the therapist's availability, he jumped on whatever was open. He booked 9:00 a.m. on Tuesday, 5:00 p.m. on Friday, 11:00 a.m. on Monday, and 4:30 p.m. on Saturday. These sessions varied in frequency, with some being between one to three weeks apart. Tia was pulled out of school and other activities to attend some of these sessions, and she missed her friend's birthday party for another. Ryan wanted Tia to have a chance to process the significant traumas she had gone through, but amid these good intentions, the need for consistency, predictability, and calm wasn't met.

As a result, Tia came to her sessions with her dad reluctantly. She was often unaware of her sessions ahead of time and was distressed about what she was missing out on. It became clear to the therapist that the lack of a consistent, predictable routine around her sessions was not setting her up to feel successful. It was also becoming a source of tension between her and her dad.

In a consultation with the therapist, Ryan was encouraged to find a time that would meet his daughter's needs as well as his own. Ryan looked ahead in the schedule and realized that in three weeks, there was a consistent spot every two weeks at 2:00 p.m. on a Thursday afternoon. He knew that he already had flexibility with his job's schedule to make Thursday work, and he also knew that Tia's school schedule would allow her to miss a bit of the afternoon in a way that would not negatively impact her academically or socially. He also knew that she didn't have other after-school activities that he would have to pull her out of. In the meantime, the counselor suggested that Ryan schedule a consult or two for himself so that he could still feel supported in knowing how to manage some of the challenging behaviors that were continuing to present themselves.

After two months of coming to therapy on a consistent day and time, Tia and Ryan were able to see a positive impact. The predictability of the sessions allowed Tia to open herself up to be vulnerable and process her emotions. Ryan came to realize that there was so much outside of the fifty-minute therapy hour that impacted the therapeutic process, and he was relieved to see how Tia benefited from the shift to a more predictable pattern.

Therapist Location

The location of a therapist's office is also worth considering in your decision. The best therapist in town may be a forty-five-minute drive from your place. If you have a child who does well in the car and the commute otherwise fits into your schedule, this might be a good fit for you. However, if your child struggles with longer car rides, it is counterproductive to put their body through that stress before each session. We have had clients who have insisted on having their child attend therapy with us because of our area of specialty—despite the long commute—and each week that child arrives in our office outside of their window of tolerance. While we can help them regulate and return to baseline, it often leaves very little time in session to process the experiences that brought them to therapy in the first place.

Virtual therapy might also be an option that works best for your family, especially if you live in a rural or remote location, you don't have a lot of flexibility in your schedule, or you (or your child) have certain physical limitations that make traveling difficult. Imagine being able to show up to session minutes after making dinner without having to wrangle a small person into putting on shoes and a jacket! In addition, some kids feel more comfortable opening up when there is a computer screen that separates them from the therapist; they feel less watched and like they can have some privacy.

However, virtual sessions have several downsides as well. Not only can technological difficulties derail an entire session, but some clients don't feel the same sense of connection that they would in a face-to-face interaction, not to mention all the distractions that you need to manage when doing therapy from your home environment. We've seen kids get pulled away from video games, play, or other preferred activities with no transition time and no change in environment to prepare their brains for a different experience. After all, it's easy for children and parents alike to be distracted by the typical commotion of a busy household.

All that said, there are times when online therapy may have therapeutic value or be the only option. In these cases, your presence and active participation in session are even more essential since the therapist is not physically in the room with you. Your therapist will probably want to spend some time with you individually before starting joint sessions to help you build the skills needed to better notice and understand the reactions your child may have in therapy. This is key so you can provide an effective container for their emotions. For example, we might say something like this to a parent whose child is starting online sessions: "You are my eyes and ears in the room. I can't see anything outside of what is on the screen. If your child is tapping their leg repeatedly during parts of the session, I won't be able to see that, but that *is* information I would want to know!"

Additional Considerations in Choosing Your Therapist

Finally, there are other trauma-related considerations to keep in mind when choosing a therapist. For example, you may find that your child has a visceral reaction to the idea of a therapist of a particular gender. While this doesn't mean you need to immediately rule out all therapists of that gender, it does mean you need to ensure that your child is going to feel safe and comfortable with whomever you choose. Similarly, some children may want to see a therapist of the same race, while others may feel triggered by this due to past experiences.

In some cases, your child may struggle to articulate the specific therapist characteristics that make them uncomfortable. They may say, "I don't know what it is, and I don't know why, but I don't like them."

Other children with less language will simply say, "I hate them." Beyond a therapist's characteristics, children may become triggered by factors you may not even have considered, such as the therapy room layout, the office location, or toys and items in the room that remind them of a previous experience. Indeed, there are a variety of triggers that may cause children with trauma to feel unsafe that would feel neutral to other people. Look through the following examples and notice if any might apply to your child.

> **Therapist and Office-Related Triggers**
>
> → A therapist who has the same name as the child's birth parent
> → A male therapist when the child is generally afraid of men
> → A therapist's particular tone of voice or voice inflection
> → An office where the child has previously received bad news from a social worker
> → An office with a particular scent or smell (for example, cleaning supplies or food)
> → The way a therapist dresses or does their makeup
> → The feeling of a blanket, sofa, or chair
> → Pretend toys, such as handcuffs, blindfolds, or medical kits
> → Sounds from a white noise or sound machine
> → Baby and family character dolls

If you notice something in this list that is likely to be a trigger for your child, you will need to decide if this trigger is likely to reduce in intensity with soothing and repetition, or if it is something that is likely to persist.

It doesn't make sense for you to spend an excessive amount of time and money working through a resistant trigger if there is another reasonable alternative. You are the best person to decide which way to go in these types of situations. Trust your gut. You know your child best.

CHAPTER 6

Engaging Your Child in the *Why* and *What* Explanation of Therapy

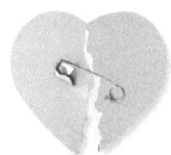

One of the biggest hurdles to starting parent-child therapy is getting your child to go with you. In these moments, you may find yourself trying to explain therapy in traditional terms by telling your child, "It helps to talk about your problems" (which provides a vague explanation that is developmentally out of their understanding) or "Sometimes you need someone besides your parents to talk to" (which is counter to our premise that *parents* need to be involved in their child's therapy). Or perhaps you've said in frustration, "I can't handle this anymore. We need to get some help with your behavior." Unfortunately, this sends a message to the child that there is something innately wrong with the way they are and interact with others. For children who have experienced significant loss, the deepest pain they feel stems from the belief "I'm not lovable," and if the idea of therapy activates this belief, they will not want to go anywhere near the experience.

If you're not sure how your child will respond to the idea of therapy, you might be wondering how to get them to cooperate with the least amount of information possible. While there is some wisdom in not overexplaining complex processes to children, it would be a mistake to market counseling to your unsuspecting child as "fun playtime." They need an explanation that fits their understanding of the world and makes sense to them. In this chapter, we'll help you walk this line between giving enough information and not too much information. This is not a conversation you want to jump into without some strategic planning. We'll also share a thing or two we've learned over the years about the language to use with children at different ages and developmental stages.

Challenges to Engaging Your Child in Therapy

There is a wide range of reactions that kids will have to the idea of seeing a therapist. Younger children may be more easily influenced by your enthusiasm for and interest in therapy but hesitant to talk with a stranger. Older children and teens may express more ambivalence or outright refusal, either stemming from anxiety, embarrassment, or a deep commitment to avoiding hard feelings. If your child is hesitant or resistant to the idea of therapy, there are a few common reasons why this may be the case.

The first is that no matter the age, it is common for kids to experience some fear of the unknown. This is especially the case for kids who have experienced trauma, as their bodies and brains will warn them that anything "unknown" is likely to be painful, unsafe, or uncomfortable. The antidote to fear, of course, is safety. Helping children move past their resistance will require an experience of felt safety—first with you and then with the therapist, which is yet another reason why your role in your child's therapy is essential. You are your child's safe place.

A second and even more compelling reason why children resist therapy happens on a more subconscious level. As humans, we are creatures of habit that resist change. That means that your child's body and brain resist change too. Your child's internal system is carefully crafted to maintain balance so they can cope with daily stressors, even if this system doesn't seem optimal or sustainable to you. Therefore, when your child resists, it is important that you honor this! That doesn't mean you throw up your hands and forget about therapy altogether. Rather, you treat your child's resistance as a clue that they are feeling overwhelmed and that you need to move slowly, providing more support before they can engage. Since it can be confusing to understand how this subconscious resistance works, let us provide you with a helpful visual as we unpack these complex systems in our minds.

Picture a precariously balanced Jenga block tower—with the blocks balanced but just barely standing because the base is almost gone. When a child has experienced developmental trauma, they develop an internal system as a result of those experiences that is intended to protect them from further harm. However, this system does not have a solid base to serve as a stabilizer. Instead, their system is balancing on one small block as opposed to a steady row of blocks. Helping your child develop a felt sense of safety is like adding blocks to their base so they have a support system that will prevent the tower from toppling over. The specifics of what that will look like will be different for every child, but you can start by being mindful of the unspoken messages you might be communicating to your child.

In particular, you want to make sure your messaging about *why* you want your child to participate in therapy doesn't inadvertently trigger feelings of shame, as shame actively works against felt safety. For example, when your child exhibits big behaviors, you might feel inclined to point to that behavior as the reason for therapy. However, think about how it would feel for you—as an adult—to be told that you need to talk to a stranger about the behaviors that your family finds difficult or confusing about you. Likewise, you need to protect a child's experience of themselves so they believe that they are whole and good, which provides a solid base for them to explore the thoughts and feelings that are hard to talk about. Felt safety is based on feeling secure, loved, worthy, valuable, and competent—and maintaining that secure base always needs to be your primary focus.

Your child may also wonder why you decided that they need trauma therapy *now*. They may have been carrying around these memories for a long time and have grown accustomed to feeling this way. They might even be convinced that this is just a part of their personality and therefore unchangeable. While it can be tricky to shift a child's viewpoint on this, we have found that using analogies can help kids understand how and why trauma memories keep coming up. For older children, we've used the analogy of a row of logs floating down the river. If you were to push one of those logs under the water, it would inevitably pop back up farther down the stream. Similarly, the body sometimes brings up a feeling or memory as a reminder of the hurt inside your child that needs healing. They may need to push those feelings back down if they aren't ready to deal with them yet, but they will resurface. In therapy, they can work toward feeling safe enough to experience these feelings so they know how to manage them the next time they surface.

For younger kids, the game of Whac-A-Mole is easier to imagine. Your child never really knows when a feeling or memory is going to surface. It might feel like just when they get one feeling under control (smack the mole down), another one pops up. While a child might continue to work at pushing each mole down as it comes up, it can be overwhelming and exhausting when it keeps happening. When they can let one come to the surface, feel it and understand it, and then return to a safe feeling in their body, they will feel better. It's a relief to be free of the frantic effort to keep them all under control.

Some older children and adolescents will insist that they are not struggling at all and do not have any upsetting thoughts, feelings, or memories. They may even go so far as to project any responsibility for their behaviors and emotions onto someone else. If your child is reacting this way, their response indicates that they are terrified to look inside. Kids who have locked down their inner world and have their walls up may not be ready to disrupt their inner systems just yet. You need to be sensitive to a teen who is showing you that looking at the past is just too much for them right now. In these cases, it may be more effective to engage them in therapy by focusing on whatever is currently hard for them. Adolescents are often willing to acknowledge sleep difficulties, social struggles, school stress, problematic romantic relationships, chronic physical discomforts, and parent-teen conflict over rules and expectations—as opposed to focusing on the past.

Balancing Power and Control

When you are devoting your time, energy, and money to therapy, it can be frustrating when your child isn't interested in attending or participating in sessions. For example, let's say your therapist has a twenty-four-hour cancellation policy, and your child insists on doing a homework assignment they need to complete that evening, making it impossible for them to attend. Or perhaps they experience a sudden onset of the worst headache they have ever had. Your younger child may even choose this as the perfect time to have a meltdown about the way you tied their shoes! All these behaviors are simply a way for your child to communicate that this is hard. Use this as an opportunity to lean in, look beneath the behavior, and practice offering *shared control* instead of setting up a situation that creates a power struggle.

The essence of trauma is the loss of control, which makes the feeling of control so important. When you realize that your child is looking for control to achieve safety, it makes it easier to understand their behavior and meet their need for control rather than battling it out. You can share control by offering developmentally appropriate choices to kids. For example, an eight-year-old who recently joined a foster family will have less trust in their foster parents to meet their needs and will need a great deal of control over what they eat, where they go, what they wear, and who tells them what to do. Similarly, consider a teenager who wants to go out after school without a supervising adult, but you know that their impulse control is much lower than what's expected of their chronological age. In this situation, you might offer to create some check-in points, set up a text messaging plan, offer to pick them up at a particular time, and provide them with a "way out" if the situation becomes overwhelming. You also want to ensure that kids have a sense of control over their own body. Forcing a child to do something with their body that challenges their own sense of safety creates a mental conundrum for them.

At the end of the day, when you look beneath the behavior and challenge your own ideas about defiance and resistance, you have more options for supporting your child. Otherwise, battles for power and control may show up when your child seems available and comfortable with counseling one week and defiantly resistant to it the next. It is understandable for your child to have less in their tank from one week to another. Understanding these shifts in behavior, instead of shaming your child for them, can build connection rather than a power struggle.

Chapter 6 | Engaging Your Child in the Why and What Explanation of Therapy

Andrew and Sam: Finding the Need Beneath Resistance

Sam came to live with her current family when she was eighteen months old. She had always struggled with sleeping, eating, and toileting. She had difficulties falling asleep and staying asleep, and she regularly experienced horrific nightmares and night terrors. She also had few foods that she could tolerate and was very particular with how her food was prepared and where she would eat it. She struggled with both daytime and nighttime incontinence as well.

At age eleven, the impact of these challenges had multiplied, causing a decline in her ability to function at school with her peers. Sam was aware of these challenges but was not able to talk about them. She would quickly deny what she was experiencing or blame it on someone else. Sam's father, Andrew, knew that she was struggling and sought out counseling services for his daughter. He explained that counseling was something they would do together, and he reassured Sam that there was no expectation for her to talk in sessions if she wasn't feeling safe or able to do so. Sam felt relieved to hear this.

After four therapy sessions, Andrew felt like they were making good traction, so he was caught off guard when Sam flat-out refused to attend session one day. Since they were past the twenty-four-hour cancellation period—and finances were tight for their family—he felt like the least Sam could do was show up. The more Andrew experienced his frustration and tried to cajole Sam into getting into the car, the worse things got. He took a moment to step back, recognize his own emotional reaction, and calm his body before continuing to engage Sam. He remembered the strategies he had learned from a parent session about what to do when your child resists coming to therapy. He approached Sam with empathy and thanked her for showing him that something was making it really hard for her to go to therapy that day. He suggested they get a snack, turn up the music, and sing during their drive. Andrew reminded Sam that counseling was something they did together and that she could choose to draw or play with the toys in the room if it felt better for her body.

Ultimately, Andrew and Sam made it to their session that day even though they were fifteen minutes late. Andrew considered it a win because he was able to really see and validate what Sam was going through, and Sam felt seen and heard by her dad. The whole experience also served as a reminder to Andrew that he needed to check in with Sam prior to sessions to see how much energy she had left in her body and to plan how he could help her get to the session.

Language That Makes Sense to Kids

Since the language you use to explain therapy to your child can make a big difference, we have put together some scripts for you to use as jumping-off points for having conversations about trauma therapy. These scripts shouldn't be used verbatim but, rather, are suggestions on how to start the conversation. You want to make sure you don't veer too far away from how you typically speak to your child so that they can relate to what you are saying. Make sure it still sounds like you! Use your intuition to decide where your child fits within these scripts and what they will best understand. For example, perhaps your sixteen-year-old has an excellent vocabulary, but when it comes to discussing emotional material, they are

Chapter 6 | Engaging Your Child in the Why and What Explanation of Therapy

at a much younger stage and would benefit from a more simplified explanation. In this case, you may choose to pull some ideas from the school-age scripts and some ideas from the teen scripts to make it work for your child.

Scripts for Infants and Toddlers

→ **Introducing the idea of counseling:** "We are going to visit a person called a counselor who has toys that we can use for special play."

→ **Explaining how counseling works:** "They will teach me how to play with you in a way that makes any yucky feelings that are stuck in your body go away. Then the counselor will watch us play and talk to us after."

→ **Offering shared control:** "You get to choose what you want to play with and how you want me to play with you. At the end, you get to decide if you want to do any talking."

Scripts for School-Age Children

→ **Introducing the idea of counseling:** "When you were little, some hard things happened. Even though you might not remember them, the feelings you got from those hard things stayed in your body. When you get upset now, your body sometimes feels those same yucky feelings from before, and that makes it harder for you to feel calm again."

→ **Explaining how counseling works:** "Coming to therapy helps these memories get unstuck from your brain and body so they don't feel scary anymore. A counselor uses toys, activities, or talking to help with the memories. When you can tell the story of the hard things that happened to you without your body having big yucky feelings, then we'll know that the memories have gotten unstuck. You will feel safe and know that it's all done. This is when counseling has done its job."

→ **Offering shared control:** "You don't have to do things that your body doesn't want to do. It's not like the dentist's office. When you have an infection in your tooth, we must take care of it right away even if it hurts a lot. With your memories, you can take your time, feel safe, and choose when you are ready."

Scripts for Teens

→ **Introducing the idea of counseling:** "I know you might not really remember the hard things that happened to you when you were much younger, but your body still stores those memories. These memories can subconsciously affect how you react in your day-to-day life. For example, when you don't feel in control of something in your life (whether it's certain household rules, curfew expectations, or homework requirements), it reminds your body of times in your childhood when you weren't in control—when unfair and unexpected things happened to you. I've been wondering if talking about some of those memories might help you feel more settled and relaxed inside."

→ **Explaining how counseling works:** "When trauma happens, it overwhelms your body, and you can't make sense of the experience, even if it happened a long time ago. It's as if you're pressing pause on a show but still experiencing the feelings of what you were watching. It's like your body feels as if that moment is still happening. Therapy is a space where you can

Chapter 6 | *Engaging Your Child in the Why and What Explanation of Therapy*

> revisit those hard experiences while feeling safe and secure. This means your hard memories get processed and resolved so your body no longer feels scared."
>
> → **Offering shared control:** "It's important for your body to feel like it has control over what happens in the counseling room. And there are many different parts of the counseling process that you get to decide about, including what information you feel comfortable sharing with the therapist and when you want to share it. When you are feeling calm and safe, we can do some of the hard work, and when you aren't feeling okay, we can focus on using skills to calm your body. If there's a day when you're not up for talking or working on anything in therapy, I can try to communicate on your behalf and talk with the counselor for you. Since you'll be right there in the room with me, if I get something wrong, you can give me a signal to try again or look for a different explanation."

In addition to using these scripts, providing your child with visual material can be helpful in familiarizing them with something unknown. For example, you might show them a photo of the counselor and the therapy room, and perhaps even the toys or materials that will be used in the session. Making the unknown more known reduces hyperarousal and opens the door to increased understanding. You can also create a visual story of going to counseling. You can sometimes do this in collaboration with the therapist, who will support you with the structure and language that will be most helpful. A good story starts and ends with a safe experience, demonstrates to the child that you will be with them, and gives important information about the *who, what, where, when,* and *why* of therapy. Appendix B contains a copy of a visual story for introducing counseling to school-age children.

If, after using all these strategies, you continue to encounter strong resistance from your child, we highly recommend that you begin the therapeutic process by attending on your own. You can view it as level one of therapy. Start by establishing a relationship with the therapist, familiarizing yourself with your role in sessions, and learning strategies to increase your child's felt sense of safety and to work through their resistance. Remember, not all the work in therapy happens in the office. In fact, with parent-child therapy, most of the change happens outside of the office. When your child begins to feel safer, you will be able to move on to level two, where they join you in sessions.

CHAPTER 7

The Parent-Therapist Alliance

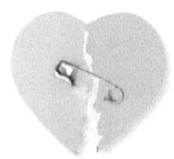

Y ou might be wondering why you would need to build a safe and trusting relationship with your child's therapist when it is your child who needs to feel safe to explore their experiences. You might also still be wondering if you *really* need to be so involved in each session. The reality is that parent-child therapy does require a level of commitment that goes beyond what you might expect from a more traditional model of child therapy. In more traditional child therapy, the counselor would work to develop what's called a "therapeutic alliance" with your child, which involves establishing a safe and secure relationship and setting some mutually agreed-upon goals for therapy. However, your participation in parent-child therapy means that both you *and* your child will be building a therapeutic alliance with the therapist.

With a strong therapeutic alliance in place, you and your child can feel safe talking about difficult or embarrassing topics and focus your time on working toward your therapy goals. That's what makes the therapeutic alliance so special: It's all about you! It's an opportunity to express yourself in a space that is free of judgment and worry. Unlike a relationship with your best friend, which requires a degree of give and take to equally consider each other's needs, your therapist is there solely for you. This is what makes the therapist-client relationship both unusual and powerful in helping you work toward your goals.

And when you think about the kind of goals your child has for therapy—to feel safe and secure in relationships, to heal from the difficult experiences they've undergone—it makes sense as to why you need to participate alongside them. These are *relational* goals that require the child's primary relational figure—you—to be part of the process. In fact, after working with hundreds of parent-child dyads over the years, we have found that the quality of the parent-therapist alliance is more important to successful treatment outcomes than the child-therapist relationship. This is why children who don't love coming to therapy (or who don't want to talk in sessions) can still experience progress in leaps and bounds. By participating in your child's therapy, you give them an opportunity to have a special experience not only with the therapist but also with you. The freedom in this protected space allows them to say exactly what they think and feel without encountering shame, disappointment, frustration, or fear. The therapist builds an alliance with you so that *you* can be part of this experience for your child as well.

Building Connection and Understanding with Your Therapist

There are several different dynamics present in the therapy room when you attend parent-child therapy. Although the relationship between you and your child is the primary focus of intervention, there is also the therapist's relationship with you, the therapist's relationship with your child, and the therapist's relationship with your parent-child relationship. Each relationship requires safety and trust, and the therapist will be intentional about creating opportunities to make this happen.

For example, to build a strong parent-therapist alliance, your therapist may ask you to attend parent-only sessions prior to starting joint therapy, and they may have you revisit these parent-only sessions at times throughout the process. That's because the parent-therapist relationship has so much power in the room. It sets the tone for how safe the child feels and creates a secure container for them to experience their emotions. If your child sees that you trust the therapist, they may find it easier to trust them as well. With more trust and felt safety, your child will be able to engage in therapy more easily and will reap its benefits.

We also start with parents because we need to assess their ability to stay regulated with their child. This is foundational work that starts before the child comes into the therapy space. For some parents, this may happen quite quickly—after a few sessions—and for other parents, this process can take months. This is not a reflection on whether you are a good or bad parent, nor is it a reflection of whether your child is simultaneously making progress during this time. In fact, your child may vicariously benefit as you learn the foundational skills you will need to be an active participant in therapy.

There are many additional therapeutic objectives parents can have for this initial phase of therapy, and what you focus on will depend a great deal on your previous experiences, your ability to regulate yourself, and how much you understand about trauma therapy. This list may appear overwhelming, but remember, there is no ideal timeline for completing any objectives other than what fits for you and your family. At the end of the day, you want to develop a solid relationship with your therapist so that when therapy gets hard, you know that they still have your best interests (and those of your child) at heart.

Objectives for the Parent-Therapist Alliance Phase of Intervention

→ Taking a baseline of your child's current functioning
→ Understanding the brain-body connection and how regulation works
→ Learn the basics of trauma therapy and what therapy will look like
→ Discovering the impact of trauma on different developmental stages
→ Learning what to realistically expect from kids
→ Exploring your beliefs about your child's behavior
→ Developing strategies to regulate yourself both in and out of session
→ Working through any difficulties you might have with taking direction, managing feedback, or trying new things in session with your child
→ Learning how to set safety-related boundaries for your child's behaviors in session
→ Exploring your own thoughts, feelings, and reactions to being in therapy
→ Working through your child's resistance to therapy
→ Targeting a few behaviors that are making daily life difficult or unsafe
→ Doing foundational attachment work to ensure your child feels safe and supported by you when they are in session
→ Learning sensory strategies to help your child feel regulated

> → Exploring hypothetical scenarios that may happen in session so you are prepared to respond therapeutically (for example, when the story you remember and tell is different from the story your child brings to therapy)

Gabriel and Annabelle: Uncovering a Need to Feel Heard and Seen

Gabriel was eager to get his daughter, Annabelle, into therapy given her challenging and often extremely hurtful behaviors. Although he was unsure of what to expect from his first parent-consultation session, the therapist took the time to really understand not only how things felt for Annabelle but also how her behaviors were impacting Gabriel and the rest of their family. Gabriel felt heard in a way that he found difficult to match in his daily life. So many of his family members and close friends had no idea what life felt like for him as he was struggling to parent his child.

As the therapist explained how Gabriel would be involved in the joint parent-child sessions, it became clear to Gabriel that he was holding a lot of animosity toward his daughter. He explained that Annabelle would often tell stories that painted him in a negative light (and that were often wildly inaccurate), which was understandably upsetting to him. As Gabriel expressed these hurts to the therapist, they both decided that he needed a few more parent-only sessions before he was ready to be in the room with Annabelle in a supportive way.

Over the next two sessions, Gabriel's therapist taught him different tools to regulate his body. They also agreed on a "secret signal" the therapist could use in session to remind

> Gabriel that the therapist understood the bigger story behind whatever version Annabelle was providing in that moment. Feeling heard by the therapist made it so much easier for Gabriel to support his daughter's big emotions (and sometimes big accusations) from a place of empathy as opposed to defensiveness.

Once you start joint sessions with your child, there may still be times when it will be helpful to have some parent-only sessions with your therapist. For example, your child may have shared a traumatic experience in session that created an intense emotional experience for you and that pushed you outside your window of tolerance, and you need to process your experience of hearing this in a parent-only session. The beauty of the therapist working with both you *and* your child is that they were in the room with you when you witnessed your child's telling of the trauma, so you don't have to re-explain it to the therapist. In this situation, the therapist can support you in feeling less overwhelmed and making hard things tolerable—much in the same way we ask you to do this for your child. Other reasons you may want to meet with your therapist alone are to:

- Better understand what your child is experiencing and what you can do to support them
- Process what a session experience was like for you emotionally, especially if you noticed any triggers or unexpected reactions
- Grieve about what your child has just shared about their experiences
- Express emotions that may not be appropriate when your child is in the room
- Recap how the therapy process is going and what gains are being made

- Keep your therapist up to date on balancing power dynamics in session
- Fill your therapist in on the many things happening in your child's life that have not come up in sessions

Your Child's Experience of the Therapy Room

When a child has experienced trauma, their brain is constantly on high alert, scanning the environment for possible danger. For this child, the therapy room is yet another unfamiliar environment that they need to assess for safety. And when they are making this assessment, they will pick up on the way you feel in the therapy room. If you feel safe, that tells their brain to feel safe. However, if you are feeling anxious or uncomfortable, your child will notice. While you might be inclined to mask your anxiety or apprehension by smiling and putting on a "happy face," your child will likely pick up on this. That is why it is so crucial for you to build the parent-therapist alliance before bringing your child into the therapy room—so you can learn how to manage any potential discomfort and confusion ahead of time.

Amber and Willow: Masking Uncomfortable Emotions

Amber has had a hard day as she arrives at therapy with her three-year-old daughter, Willow, who has a history of being hesitant to engage in the therapy room. Willow notices her mother's discomfort and repeatedly asks, "Mom, are you okay?" Amber knows her daughter is anxious about participating in therapy and responds with overexaggerated positive emotions that she thinks will show her child that everything is okay. She puts on a wide smile, speaks in an overly cheery tone, and places several therapy toys in front of Willow in an attempt to get her excited about therapy today.

Willow is stressed by her mother's behaviors, which don't match the feelings she is picking up on. Willow reaches for a toy bottle and attempts to put it in Amber's mouth. She is trying to soothe her mother. She knows that something is wrong, but her mother is acting like it isn't. Amber tries to draw Willow toward the artificial experience she is trying to create, but Willow won't accept the invitation because it doesn't feel right. Willow's behavior escalates as she expresses her distress, which leads Amber to feel more exhausted and frustrated. She is inadvertently passing along her coping strategy, which is to mask her true emotions rather than express what she is genuinely feeling.

Since Amber has a safe and trusting relationship with the therapist, the therapist takes time to draw Amber's attention to her own dysregulation and reminds her of the strategies she must use to calm her own emotions so she can be present in a genuine way.

As Amber's story illustrates, we sometimes need a reminder to care for our own bodies and brains so that we can show up authentically in our interactions with others. By building a strong therapeutic alliance with your therapist in advance of joint sessions, you can learn how to tune in to yourself, notice any dysregulation, and reorient yourself with the strategies you've learned. Remember that when we ask children to explore their most difficult memories, there will always be some fear attached to this process. Your desire to protect your child from painful experiences is in direct conflict with the need for them to revisit these memories to heal.

Developing a clear plan for your own regulation in session will help you to feel prepared for the process.

Navigating Your Own Emotions in Therapy

In parent-child therapy, the therapy room is not a space for parents to express and process their own experiences. They are acting as a container and co-regulator for their child to do this work. However, it is natural and expected that you will have your own emotional experiences in session that will require processing as well. If you delay processing these experiences (or don't process them at all), the emotional intensity can start to feel too overwhelming, and you may be tempted to skip or "forget" to schedule the next appointment. Trauma therapy is heavy. It's asking you to make space in your brain and body for your child's hurt. When you witness a loved one process something painful, it will create a similar experience inside your body whether you are able to recognize it or not.

For example, one of our clients would often find himself needing a nap later in the day after his son's therapy sessions. Not realizing that this was his body's reaction to the experience of observing his son's pain, he considered it a strange coincidence that he was always in need of a nap on Monday afternoons. If he hadn't had an opportunity to process his own experiences in parent-only sessions, he may not have recognized what was happening in his body. The goal was to notice, label, and release these experiences so he was no longer carrying the burden of his son's pain.

If you are spending a great deal of time in session listening to your child's story without expressing your own thoughts and feelings, we highly recommend journaling after the session is over. One option is to engage in unstructured or open-ended journaling. Simply think about the session, remember what it felt like in your body, set a timer for five minutes, and start writing. Don't worry about spelling, punctuation, or grammar—just write whatever comes to mind. You can keep it to reflect on later or dispose of it immediately. Alternatively, you can use more structured journaling prompts to process key elements of the session. The following is a sample template you can use for this purpose.

> ### Journal Template Example
>
> 1. Write about a time when you felt activated during your child's session.
>
>   Example: *I felt dysregulated when my child began speaking about an experience of abuse that I was completely unaware of, which had happened when she was in her previous foster home.*
>
> 2. Unpack the following experiences.
>
>   → Sensations: What did it feel like in your body?
>
>   Example: *I felt tightness in my chest, rapid breathing, and a desire to get out of the room.*
>
>   → Emotions: What feelings came up for you?
>
>   Example: *I felt overwhelmed and helpless.*
>
>   → Thoughts: What were you thinking?
>
>   Example: *I found myself thinking that I wanted my child to stop talking. I was trying to rationalize what she was saying and telling myself that because she wasn't emotional when she told the story, it wasn't much of a big deal. And yet I had other competing thoughts—like "How did I not know this?" "Is she making this up?" and "What does this mean for her future?"—because I knew how deep this experience had to have been for her, and I*

was panicked at the thought that there might be more traumas in her life that I don't know about.

3. Have you ever felt like this before in your life?

    Example: I felt like this before when I found out that my older sister, who was fourteen years old at the time, was engaging in cutting. I was just six years old when I walked into her room and saw the cuts she was making on her arms. I felt overwhelmed and helpless. My big sister was my world! My sister tried to convince me that it was not a big deal and that I did not need to worry or tell our parents about it. I realize I have not thought of this memory for over two decades, but it felt so real as I was recalling it.

4. How will your new insights impact your relationship with your child and your life moving forward?

    Example: After taking time to calm my body, I recognize the root of my behavior and no longer feel as overwhelmed. I was able to talk it through with a good friend and then booked a session with my therapist. Being able to process this memory has allowed me to be present with my child and no longer hold an underlying fear that something might pop up in session that I won't be able to manage. After taking time to soothe my younger self, I can now sit in the counseling room with confidence that I can manage big, unexpected news about people I love without feeling stuck in this memory from when I was six.

Challenges in the Parent-Therapist Alliance

If you've had less-than-ideal experiences with therapists in the past, you may be feeling hesitant to trust another one. Or if you've never tried therapy before, it might feel like it's too much work to develop a trusting relationship with someone you've never met before. Maybe you struggle with the desire to take the lead in therapy and find it difficult to trust that the therapist has a plan. If you are a bit of a type A personality, you might be able to relate to this right away. Or maybe you're worried the therapist will think that your child's behaviors are your fault or the result of poor parenting. After all, it feels terrible to be judged when you are trying your best. You may also feel like therapy requires a lot of time and energy when the issues you are facing need a faster solution.

All these experiences are legitimate, and there are no easy answers for them. How do you trust someone who doesn't know your child as well as you do? How tough is it to see that your child is feeling scared and not shut the process down to spare them the pain? How hard is it to know that your child has forgotten to mention some details of the story and not jump in right away to give a fuller picture? As therapists who have worked with countless families (and especially Andrea, who has attended therapy with her own children), we feel this to our core. If any of these examples sound like you, be open with your therapist throughout the process and don't be afraid to acknowledge what's happening inside of you and to ask your therapist for help if you begin feeling overwhelmed or are unable to remain regulated during the process.

In addition, it is not uncommon for parents to feel like therapy is taking too long and detracting from resources that would go toward other important obligations. It can be difficult to trust that the therapist is not taking advantage of your resources by suggesting a longer process. This is a tough one. If you are feeling this way, you and your therapist need to have an honest and clear conversation so you feel confident in (and can make choices about) the frequency and length of treatment. In addition, if you're worried that having extra parent-only sessions will prolong therapy as a whole, rest assured that in the long run, this allows you to continue supporting your child long after therapy has concluded.

Another common, but unexpected, experience that many parents have is feeling jealous when they observe the way their child interacts with the therapist. Perhaps this has been your own experience when you notice your therapist's incredible ability to empathize with your child and say just the right thing to reduce their distress. In these moments, you might find yourself thinking that your therapist would make a better parent. This is especially the case if you never had the chance for this kind of reparative experience in your own childhood—a chance to express yourself without fear of abandonment, loss, or repercussions. Even though the rational side of your brain knows you shouldn't feel jealous, the emotional side of your brain nonetheless feels like this is unfair: *How can my child act so terribly and have someone kindly understand and make sense of their behavior for them? No one did that for me.* It is common for parents to discover things like this about themselves when they are engaging in parent-child therapy. The key is to notice your reaction without judgment and then reach out for help from your therapist. Knowing that these feelings of jealousy are normal can alleviate a great deal of stress and help you stay engaged in the process. (And trust us, as therapists, we aren't looking to become parents to any more kids. We already struggle to apply what we know in our own homes!)

However, it is still possible that, after seeing a therapist for some initial sessions, you decide that they are not a good fit for you and your child. Maybe they don't seem to prioritize the behavior that you really want to address in session. Maybe they have a different idea of what it means to triage the difficult behaviors you are dealing with at home. Or perhaps they just exhibit certain relational characteristics that you find annoying. If this is the case, know that it is perfectly okay to seek out another therapist. It is so important for you to believe in the work you are doing in therapy and to trust your counselor to guide you through this process. There will be times when you feel frustrated, disappointed, or misunderstood in parent-child sessions, and you need a foundation of trust to fall back on to work through these tough moments.

If all this talk about the parent-therapist alliance sounds like a lot of work, it can be. But we want to encourage you to consider the benefits of this alliance as well. By developing a solid working relationship with your therapist, you are giving yourself an opportunity to feel deeply supported and understood—which, in turn, allows you to be with your child in their hardest experiences. Even more profound is the opportunity for you and your child to both experience healing of present and past experiences.

CHAPTER 8

Setting the Relational Foundation for Effective Therapy

Although most therapists are happy to support you in getting ready to engage in trauma therapy, if you prefer a little more of a DIY approach, this chapter discusses how to prepare yourself and your family so you can make the most of your time in the counseling office. Maybe we can save you a few bucks too. It all starts with learning the foundational skills of therapeutic parenting. If this language is new to you, you might be wondering, *What is therapeutic parenting? Isn't therapy what you have a therapist for? What do you mean I need to do this at home? I'm not trained. I don't know what I'm doing.* The amazing thing about being a parent is that you are there 24/7. Unless you are ready to house your therapist and create a suite for them in your basement, they are not going to be there every time things get tricky. Trust us, we have had many requests for this, and we say no every time. The day-to-day stuff is all you!

As you'll learn in this chapter, therapeutic parenting isn't some type of therapy prep work; it's a way of being with, relating to, and responding to your child that prioritizes connection and safety over everything else.

If you are well versed in therapeutic parenting and your parent-child relationship foundation feels solid, we still have a few ideas for you in this chapter. If you are far from therapeutic parenting or have no idea what it is, we can set you on the right path. You can use the information in this chapter like a checklist or thermometer to measure how well you are doing with this foundational skill. Although it can feel overwhelming to think of yourself as being therapeutic in your own home—*Am I really expected to pull this off unsupervised?*—we hope by the end of this chapter, you are feeling more empowered than scared to set the foundation for therapy by being a therapeutic parent.

Therapeutic Parenting: Four Practical Steps to Set the Foundation

The basic cornerstone of therapeutic parenting is *attunement*, which is the process of noticing and responding to your child's needs at any given moment. Attunement requires the ability to "read" your child's emotional and behavioral cues—looking for their reactions, body language, words, and vocal signals—to know what they might be thinking and feeling. It's a deeper and wider version of empathy that allows your child to feel truly *known* by you. Attunement is supposed to start in infancy, when a parent meets an infant's basic needs for food, sleep, safety, and love. When this doesn't happen in those critical early years, children's cues become disorganized, which is why kids with a trauma history need caregivers who will persist long enough through trial and error until they can read their child's cues and respond confidently. The experience of being "known" is a powerful connector that they need in order to feel safe and secure.

The idea of attunement can feel like a hard task to take on, especially when your child is exhibiting big behaviors, which is why we've broken down this concept into manageable to-dos. In particular, we have developed four steps you can follow to move you toward attunement. Each step might take days or weeks to practice. Some might come easier to you than others. We recommend you work through the steps sequentially. Notice if you feel the urge to skip over one or have thoughts like *That won't work for my kid* or *I already do that*. There is always room for growth in any relationship, particularly with your children.

Step 1: Start with Noticing and Curiosity

When your child exhibits behaviors that seem to come out of nowhere and that you don't understand, use this as an opportunity to get curious. Practice noticing all the things that happened before, during, and after the behavior, including any nonverbal communication between you and your child. Think of yourself as a detective in this phase. You aren't really *doing* anything different; you are just *observing* things that you didn't notice before by getting curious. In her book *Beyond Behaviors*, which offers a neuroscience-based approach to managing children's behavioral challenges, Mona Delahooke (2019) says, "When we see a behavior that is problematic or confusing, the first questions we should ask isn't 'How do we get rid of it?' but rather 'What is this telling us about the child?'" (p. 11). It can feel so good for children and youth to experience someone being curious about, rather than frustrated with or upset by, their behavior.

As a disclaimer, getting curious doesn't mean you ask your child questions. That would put the responsibility on your child to explain themselves, which is an ineffective strategy most of the time. If you are unsure whether your observation skills are on track, make statements rather than asking questions. For example, let's say your child comes home from school angry and defiant with no apparent cause. You notice their slumped body language, harsh tone of voice, lack of eye contact, and avoidance of physical contact. A noticing statement could sound like "It seems like you had a hard day today." Your child might be surprised that you responded with curiosity and concern rather than correcting or punishing their behavior. It may allow your child to access a softer place inside where they can ask for help when something is hard.

Noticing can go beyond what is happening in the present moment as you draw on your knowledge of the past and the future. For example, you might notice a change in your child's mood and recognize that this shift is quite common this time of year. Or noticing can take you into the future when you recognize that your child's incredible meltdown happened on the way to grandma and grandpa's house, where they will be spending the night away from you.

If you find the practice of noticing to be difficult, you may be quite dysregulated in your own body. Your dysregulation may be a reaction to your child's behavior. We've all been there! Try taking some deep breaths, get some water, shift your position, and remind yourself, *I'm choosing to practice curiosity in this moment so I can help my child.* As you do this day after day, it will start to feel more natural and require less energy. We also recommend you get into the habit of keeping track of what you notice. You will need this once you get to the third step of this skill (drawing connections). In appendix C, we have provided a checklist you can use to keep track of what you notice. While increasing your ability to notice your child and understand their experience is not a magic cure for everything, it does have the power to completely change the way you view your child and how you feel about the aspects of parenting that are hard. It's a risky business because you will *feel* more when you are attuned. The benefits, though, far outweigh the cost.

Chapter 8 | *Setting the Relational Foundation for Effective Therapy*

Randall and Adam: Noticing and Curiosity

Adam was a twelve-year-old boy who had always demonstrated big reactions to seemingly small things. When he was younger, his behaviors were easier to manage because he was smaller, and his behaviors were still seen within the normal range for children his age. However, as he got older, his big responses grew alongside him. His voice was louder, he was more destructive, his language was more abrasive, and he often ran away. Adam's father, Randall, never really knew why Adam was reacting the way he did, but he had a general idea that he was dysregulated.

Randall's consistent response to these outbursts throughout the years was to quickly distract Adam and then avoid talking about it for fear of setting Adam off again. Randall had never had a conversation with Adam about his big emotions, and he was unclear on how Adam viewed them. One thing was clear, though: Over time, Randall had grown less patient and more frustrated with Adam when he reacted in these ways.

After Randall's initial parent intake session with his therapist, he was given homework to practice using the four steps to gain a better understanding of Adam's confusing behavior. At first, Randall was hesitant and skeptical. He truly felt like his son's behaviors came out of nowhere, and he had a hard time believing that stepping back and noticing would illuminate any hidden clues. But he knew that what he was currently doing wasn't helping, so he thought he would give it a try.

As Randall began with the first step of noticing and approaching his son with curiosity, he realized that Adam's big emotions showed up around mealtimes, bedtimes, and transitions to places outside of the home. Randall continued to keep an eye on these situations to look for any other clues. He also saw that Adam was very reactive when interacting with a certain group of friends. Randall took the time outside of these big reactions to be curious. He found himself wondering what it was about these times that made Adam so dysregulated. He also started to wonder how Adam's early experiences were impacting his current responses. Was there something scary about bedtime? Was he trying to protect himself with these explosive responses? Something about food or mealtimes was upsetting to him, and spending time with his peers must have been hard for him on some level too.

Step 2: Practice Empathy

Now that your curiosity has been piqued and you have sharpened your noticing skills, we are going to move on to step 2. Let's start by making sure you are on the same page about what empathy is. In a general sense, empathy involves being able to take on another person's perspective so that you can understand what they may be thinking or feeling. In the context of therapeutic parenting, empathy involves letting your child know (whether through your words or your body language) that you recognize when they are going through a difficult experience and that you are in that experience with them. This is different from just knowing they are having a hard time, as empathy is more of a *feeling* response than a *thinking* response. The previous practice you have done with noticing—allowing you to really see what's happening with your child—will make it easier for you to feel connected to their experience.

Importantly, empathy allows you to accept your child's experience even when it doesn't make sense to you. That's because when you sit beside someone who is hurting, you often have a similar feeling of sadness or pain.

This is how mirror neurons work. Your brain is triggered to feel something the other person is feeling by simply observing their experience. When it comes to a child who has experienced trauma, we have found that simply offering that child empathy will often resolve patterns of dysregulation that have otherwise persisted. It has the power to end repetitive behavior. When you aren't sure how to name an experience your child is having, but you want to be empathic, you can start by noticing and commenting on their discomfort. They may be feeling confused or exhausted, or their engine may be running high, which often manifests as frenetic energy. Saying this out loud with empathy helps them feel like you are really with them. It says, "I see you" and "I got you." Showing a child you believe them in this way is the fastest route to connection.

However, empathy can be particularly challenging when your child's behavior creates an emotional response in you. Meltdowns in toy stores are one of our favorite examples. It's even worse when your local grocery store has a toy section conveniently situated between the front entrance and the bathroom. Even if your child has literally never seen or heard of a toy before today, the intensity of their demand makes it seem like it is essential to their survival. As you respond with the dreaded word *no*— perhaps rationalizing why this is something you can't purchase today—this activates a bigger reaction in your child that starts with pleading, moves toward yelling, and quickly shifts into a full meltdown. Out of sheer desperation, you might shift your approach and use bribery, negotiation, or threats, depending on your parenting style—none of which are going to create a peaceful ending to this scenario.

If you have enough perspective, either in the moment or upon reflecting later, you can notice that the intensity of your child's response doesn't seem to match the situation. You're not allowing them to take home a $45 stuffie, yet their body is acting as though they are fending off an attacker. For children with a history of trauma, small discomforts and disappointments such as this register as danger in the brain. It reminds them of past times in their lives when trusted adults failed to meet their needs. Remembering this makes it easier to understand your child's meltdown and respond in an empathic and soothing manner.

Randall and Adam: Offering Empathy at Bedtime

As Randall started getting curious about Adam's dysregulation, he recognized that he had never stopped to consider what bedtime felt like for Adam. While Randall still wasn't sure what the solution was to these big outbursts, he could clearly see that Adam was struggling and in distress. He voiced this to Adam by saying, "Buddy, I can see how hard this is for you right now. Something about bedtime is making you feel awful. I am so sorry this is so tough right now." Randall admitted that it was not natural for him to sit with these big feelings, especially since it didn't resolve things immediately. However, what it did do was allow Adam to feel seen and validated. Adam quickly noticed that his dad was responding in a "weird" way, and he started to nod his head in agreement as his dad continued to name how hard this must be for Adam.

Step 3: Draw Connections

After getting into the habit of noticing and offering empathy, it is not uncommon to experience feelings of guilt, regret, and sadness that you didn't notice these things sooner. You may wonder if you missed opportunities to understand and respond with empathy along the way. You may also have some thoughts about how your previous responses aggravated or exaggerated your child's dysregulation. We know this is hard. We've been there ourselves and have sat beside many parents who have these feelings. It is important to remember that you were doing the best you could with what you knew at the time. You didn't know any better, but now you do. We encourage you to talk to someone you trust (or to write in your journal) and then release your feelings around this.

We also encourage you to take the opportunity to make amends. Children are never too young to experience a parent who wholeheartedly wants to repair something that potentially harmed the relationship. This can be hard to do, particularly if you never experienced this as a child. Saying "I'm sorry" and sitting with this discomfort is an important skill. Once you've made amends, you can move onward and upward. You have a new level of insight and you are ready to try some new responses, which brings us to the fourth step.

Randall and Adam: Making Connections Between Past and Present

After a few weeks, Randall was starting to see that there were patterns in Adam's big behaviors. Randall knew that Adam had significant trauma around separations earlier in life, yet he hadn't considered that bedtime would feel like a significant separation until now. He also knew that Adam had occasional nightmares, which could explain where some of the fear of going to bed was coming from. Randall continued to reflect on how his view of his son's behaviors was shifting. In the past, he hadn't realized that Adam's aggressive and angry reactions stemmed from fear and anxiety, and he was now making up for the many opportunities he missed to help Adam become more regulated.

Step 4: Try New Responses

Now that you have built some noticing habits, flexed your empathy muscles, and made some connections, you are ready to try out responding differently to your child. This will be a bit like learning a new language, so it's going to feel awkward at first. Your child may make you feel even more clumsy or uncomfortable by saying things like "Why are you talking like that?" or "That isn't the real you." Kids love to call their parents out! Changes can be unsettling for everyone, even when it's a good type of change. You will need to have some resilience to get through this stage. Stick with it until it starts to feel comfortable and natural.

Here are a few examples of how you might respond differently to a variety of behavioral challenges:

- When your child is exhibiting big externalizing behaviors: "I notice that whenever you come home from school, you have so many yucky feelings inside that you hit, yell, and say mean things to try to get it all out. I think school is hard for you and you need a way to feel better when you come home. I would like to try some new things to help you feel better in your body. Tomorrow when I pick you up, let's go to a playground before we go home."

- When you have asked your child to do something repeatedly and they not only avoid doing it but also don't acknowledge the request and seem pleased with your frustration: "I can see that when I remind you to empty the dishwasher [*child's daily chore*], you really don't want to do it. Something inside you just tries to ignore that I'm even asking you so you don't have to get upset. You are hoping to avoid doing it *and* avoid having an argument about it. I know that both are hard for you."

- When your child is lashing out with anger and criticism because you are trying to correct them for an unacceptable behavior: "I notice that when we talk about something you did wrong, you feel super anxious and uncomfortable and want to get rid of that feeling as soon as possible. When you said those angry things to me yesterday, I think you wanted me to take some of the blame for what happened so that you wouldn't feel so bad. It's hard to feel that way, and you get worried that it will last forever. Getting angry is really your way of protecting yourself."

Although it can feel counterintuitive to respond in these ways, we guarantee that once you try this and find the magic in it, you will be hooked and use it all the time. Remember that it's okay to sound awkward and unsure when you are trying out something new. In addition, notice that none of these examples solve the problem at hand (more on that later), but they do shift the focus away from punishment and shame to empathy and understanding instead. This helps your child get back to a baseline level of calm before you move into problem-solving. This is the beginning of a new pattern of responding to your child.

Randall and Adam:
New Responses at Bedtime

As Randall made the connection between bedtime and Adam's fear of separation, he responded differently the next time Adam acted out at bedtime: "I notice that bedtimes are really hard, and I wonder if being away from me feels scary." He noticed how awkward it felt to say this sentence out loud, even though he believed what he was saying. It just wasn't the typical way he would converse with Adam, particularly at bedtime.

Although Adam didn't magically settle in for a peaceful night's sleep without a fuss, he did make eye contact with Randall, and the energy between them shifted just for a

> moment. With time, Randall's new way of responding started to feel more familiar and natural. The idea that Adam wasn't defiant—he was scared—changed Randall's view of the problem, and it motivated him to respond differently. Randall moved toward bedtime with the intention of creating safety and connection to soothe the fear that he finally realized was at the root of the big behaviors.

Readiness Assessment of the Parent-Child Relationship

Back in chapter 3, we discussed the importance of doing your own inner work so you can be present with your child while they do theirs. We looked at the different aspects of readiness, including your ability to manage big behaviors in the therapy room, follow your therapist's lead, regulate your own body, and hold on to your own emotional experience when it may interfere with your child's processing. In this section, we now want you to consider the readiness of your *parent-child relationship*. These are foundational experiences that need to be in place for trauma therapy to be effective. Let's have a look at where you are at with these four key readiness assessment factors:

- **Your child can take direction from you for the purposes of safety.** This can look different depending on a child's age, developmental stage, temperament, prior counseling experience, and ability to articulate their own needs. In general, though, a child should be able to follow basic safety directions from you. This is important to ensure that your child can be safe with others who might be in the counseling office waiting area, be safe with their own body if the counseling office is adjacent to a roadway

Chapter 8 | *Setting the Relational Foundation for Effective Therapy*

or parking lot, and protect the privacy of any other families also participating in therapy at the same time.

- **You are able to read your child's cues most of the time.** This is not about being perfect, as every situation will have unique characteristics that make it easier or harder to read your child's cues. It's about being confident in your ability to accurately interpret your child's thoughts and feelings. Children who have experienced trauma put out confusing signals that require more time and effort to interpret. You do not have to be 100 percent on point. It is a general feeling that you can do this most of the time.

- **Your child demonstrates that they can accept co-regulation from you.** This doesn't mean they can regulate easily or quickly, just that they can accept your presence in their distress. This is usually evident in the way your child looks to you for comfort and safety. Trauma therapy asks your child to dig deep into their most painful experiences, and they need comfort and security to do that. If your child is not in a place where they feel like they can turn to you in their distress, you are putting them in an incredibly vulnerable position to look at hard memories all on their own. The therapist's role is to create a safe space for the relationship, while your role is to create a safe space for your child.

- **Both you and your child understand the basic *why* and *what* of trauma therapy.** Your child's understanding will depend on their chronological age and developmental capacity. We recommend returning to chapter 6 and revisiting the explanations and scripts that help children of different ages and stages understand the *why* and *what* of trauma therapy.

When these readiness factors are present in the parent-child relationship, your child can be soothed by you and can work through any discomfort or fear in sessions instead of developing a negative association with the therapy room or the therapist's presence. It is a beautiful thing to witness a child experience discomfort from a memory or current experience, notice their own feelings, and immediately turn to their parent for comfort. The more natural and comfortable this feels for both you and your child, the more quickly your child can transition into processing their traumas. Although it's helpful when kids have some insight into the connection between their past experiences and their current difficulties, this isn't necessary for them to be ready. Often, the process of explaining how therapy works is enough. If your child trusts that you have their best interests in mind, can be soothed by you, and accepts your presence in the room, that is ready enough.

Jayden and Raquel: Assessing Readiness for Therapy

Jayden began attending therapy with his mother, Raquel, shortly after he was placed in their home. During the intake session with Raquel, the therapist was extremely concerned about Jayden's well-being due to the severe nature of his symptoms. She immediately set up a joint therapy appointment with Jayden and Raquel, who was at her wits' end with trying to manage his impossible behaviors. This all happened so quickly that the therapist didn't conduct an adequate readiness assessment, as she was having a reactionary response to Jayden's needs. This can happen even among seasoned therapists, who want to help preserve foster placements and keep kids safe.

Jayden arrived at the first therapy session with his foster mom, who appeared to have no ability to offer direction and had to work very hard just to get him through the clinic's front door. He immediately started opening all the doors in the waiting room, likely needing to assure himself there wasn't any danger on the other side. This disrupted multiple therapy sessions that other families were having, and it created a feeling of frustration for other clients in the waiting room. Once inside the therapy room, Jayden pulled everything off the walls and then proceeded to grab a crayon and draw on them, pausing only to throw objects directly at the therapist. Raquel was devastated by the destruction and her own lack of ability to prevent the behavior. She left that day feeling out of control and confused about how this was supposed to help.

Without an adequate readiness assessment, Jayden was introduced too quickly to an environment that he did not yet feel safe in. A different introduction to the therapy room would have helped him leverage the safety he felt with his foster mother to set him up for success. It will take a great deal of work after this incident to help him have a different experience in the future.

As Jayden's example illustrates, we strongly believe in not asking kids to do things in therapy that they don't yet have the foundational skills to tolerate. Otherwise, we risk introducing kids to therapy and it not "working" because they lack these foundational skills. This can lead kids to develop a resistance to counseling or "help." They develop a story in their minds that counseling doesn't work for them, so they avoid going so they can avoid feeling unsuccessful. We've worked with countless adults who have carried the story of "counseling doesn't work for me" throughout their entire lives because they had an unfortunate experience as a child or teenager. If your child is participating in interventions that they don't believe in (or they are being "voluntold" to attend therapy), it's a good idea to step back and reassess your and your child's readiness for trauma therapy.

Assessing readiness can be trickier with an older child who asks for counseling but has not yet learned to take direction or receive soothing from their primary caregiver. We find that these are the times when parents are really tempted to drop off their kids and have their kids develop an independent relationship with the therapist to respect their privacy. While kids can learn some helpful skills from a therapist, we don't recommend that they engage in trauma therapy without the foundational attachment relationship in place.

You might be surprised to learn that pushback from a child of any age is not necessarily indicative of a lack of readiness. Instead, you want to recognize their pushback as a form of communication and get curious about what is creating this resistance. Often, you'll find their resistance stems from a fear of the unknown and, particularly with regard to counseling, a fear of having no escape from difficult feelings. However, if the resistance you are encountering feels too much and too hard to manage, or you don't understand it, we recommend you begin the therapeutic process at home first. Return to the strategies in chapter 6, remembering that not all the work in therapy happens in the office. When your child begins to feel safer, they will be ready to join you in session.

CHAPTER 9

Preparing for the Impact of Therapy on Family Life

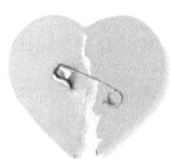

The family is a system that has a specific way of functioning (Satir et al., 2006). Think of your family of origin. Whether it was dysfunctional or not, it operated within a set of patterns that repeated themselves over time until everyone accepted that's the way it was. Until something threatens to interfere with the system, we often don't think about it; we just operate within it. Sometimes, though, we forget that even adding something positive to the system can put pressure on it and create a ripple effect. We see this in families who bring their children to therapy. As things begin to shift in the parent-child relationship, another child in the family begins to externalize the traumatic experiences they have been subconsciously holding. For many parents, this can be surprising and unsettling, and they may misinterpret therapy as being the problem when it simply reflects an inevitable change in the family system.

At the same time, remember that your child needs the container of the family system functioning effectively to sustain the changes they make in therapy. This may mean pausing or shifting a therapeutic approach to ensure that changes don't happen ahead of what the system can tolerate.

This is particularly relevant in families with multiple children with trauma histories. We recommend using your parent-only sessions as an opportunity to talk about the impact of changes on other members of the family. Although you may feel hesitant to bring up concerns about the family system in case that will hinder your child's progress, it's okay to ask for something the system needs.

If the idea that therapy will impact the whole system feels overwhelming, take some time to decide how you will create space for this to happen. Remember, slow is fast when it comes to trauma therapy. If you move too quickly, it's hard for the system to sustain the changes. It's best to make shifts at the speed that your family can tolerate.

Preparing Other Children in the Family

You may have noticed that kids have questions about *everything*. Their questions may come from a place of curiosity or the need for security and predictability in their world. Without explanations, children will fill in the blanks with whatever seems to make the most sense to them in the moment. If other children in your family have questions about therapy, we recommend that you avoid disclosing too much information about the child who will be attending sessions while offering enough explanation to satisfy their siblings' curiosity. What they are really after is how this change might affect their world and how they will continue to get their needs met.

You might want to talk about this in a gradual way, starting with a basic explanation and waiting to see if they need more. You can start with a statement like "You might be wondering why Mommy and your sister are seeing a counselor." Pause to see if you have some engagement and, if so, proceed: "Counselors are grown-ups who help children and parents understand and feel better about hard things that have happened." Next, let them know what will change. Think practically about how their daily schedule will be affected, and encourage them to let you know if something is hard: "Every Tuesday after dinner, your sister and I will drive to the counselor's office, spend one hour there, and then come home. You will be at home with Grandma and your younger brother. This means that Grandma will be the one to play and read with you while we are gone. I will be home before you go to bed. If you have any big feelings about me being gone, please tell me and I will try to help you with them."

You might get some pushback if your other kids are worried that this change will lead to an imbalance of attention and special privileges. If you are parenting more than one child with early trauma, there might be some questions or feelings about what's fair, who is more special, and who has been through harder things. These are all normal worries, and you will have more success if you focus your energy on empathizing with and understanding their point of view rather than going on a futile mission to ensure that everything is exactly equal. We often say to parents that fairness in a family is making sure that everyone feels safe and has their needs met. This is going to look different for each family member. We suggest offering choices that give your other children some control over how they get their needs met: "I understand it's hard that your sister gets to have time with me after dinner when we are usually all together. It's even harder to know that we might stop to get a snack on the way and you aren't there to get one. I want to plan a special time for you and me too. Would you like to do that while your sister is at dance class, or would you like me to pick you up an hour early from school?" The combination of empathy and choice supports connection and safety even when things don't seem fair.

Managing External Expectations and Demands During Therapy

We want you to recognize that therapy is going to take up space in the family. As a parent, you can only hold so much, so it's important to take a good assessment of everything on your "family plate" and "individual plate" to ensure that there is space available for this. It's not the same as taking up a new sport where you drop your child off at 4:00 p.m., pick them up at 6:30 p.m., and then continue with your evening routine. Trauma therapy is not just one hour of session and thirty minutes of driving. The *before*, *during*, and *after* emotional requirements make trauma therapy more demanding. Therefore, you want to ask yourself if there is something you can take off your plate for a period of time—not forever—to make this process more manageable. Here are some questions to ask yourself so you can temporarily lighten your load:

- Are you able to make any changes to your work schedule?
- Do you have a volunteer role that you could suspend temporarily?
- Are you able to access support with household chores (for example, cooking, cleaning, or laundry)?
- Is there someone close to your family who would love to spend some time with the children who are not in therapy and provide them with more attention?
- Is there someone who can drive your other kids to their extracurricular activities that would alleviate some of your time spent on the road?
- Is there anything else you typically do to support others (for example, babysitting your brother's kids every Wednesday and

volunteering for the hot lunch program at school) that you could take some time away from while you focus on therapy?

- Are there any self-demands that you can step away from temporarily to allow yourself extra space (for example, taking a break from hosting Thanksgiving dinner or deciding that one day a week your family eats takeout rather than a home-cooked meal)?

There may be times in your life when there is no space for therapy. That's okay. In these cases, you can just use this opportunity to work on the strategies discussed in chapter 8 to strengthen your attunement while you work toward creating space for therapy. It may take some time to step away from your current commitments or ensure that the urgent needs of other family members are taken care of. This is healthier than insisting your child go to trauma therapy without making enough space for it to be successful.

Choosing a Parent to Take the Lead

Just as the whole family system can shift when a child begins therapy, so, too, can the parenting system experience change from this experience. Our model of trauma therapy typically involves having only one parent and one child in the room at a time. That's because children who have been traumatized are already on edge, constantly watching and reading the cues of each adult in the room. When you include the therapist, there will already be two adults in the room. Including any more detracts from the child's ability to focus on their own experience in session. Another problem with having two parents in the room is that different opinions will inevitably come up, with a limited opportunity to resolve them. (This is not couples therapy, after all.) When parents are not on the same page, a child might move into the role of peacekeeper or feel responsible for the frustration or disagreement. These types of conversations are best kept within parent sessions, which both parents are welcome to attend regardless of who is supporting the child in session.

When deciding on which parent will attend sessions, it's important to keep in mind that the child may feel more comfortable disclosing certain types of experiences with one parent over the other. This can be, but is not always, related to attachment security. Naturally, a more secure and stable parent-child relationship reduces hypervigilance and offers the safety needed for some kids to disclose their experiences. However, there are times when other factors are at play. For example, consider a child who was placed with his adoptive family at the age of six. Prior to his adoption, his birth mother requested to meet only his adoptive mother, as she didn't feel comfortable around men who were strangers. This child may prefer that his adoptive mother attend sessions, as she has had direct experiences with his birth mom that make it easier for him to share his feelings of loss. As another example, consider a kid who was often touched inappropriately by a female relative who babysat her when her parents were at work. When it comes time to work through these traumatic experiences, the child may be adamant that her dad be the one to attend sessions with her.

If you are co-parenting with someone that you don't live with or are no longer in a relationship with, the decision about who will attend therapy may be more complicated. If you are on good terms and operate as a parenting team, you will simply make this decision based on the same criteria as a parenting couple. If you are not on good terms (and you are reading this book because *you* are the parent who will be supporting your child), consider how you can keep the other parent informed. It may feel more comfortable for them to receive updates directly from the therapist. If it isn't possible to even keep them informed, you must at the very least have their consent or have appropriate legal documentation that allows you to make independent decisions related to the child's medical care.

If you are in a situation where your home or family environment is volatile or contentious, you and your child will benefit from working with a therapist who can first support you in creating safety and connection before you begin trauma therapy. It's okay to wait on helping your child process historical trauma until they have a safe base from which to do this. As a parent, you also need to feel safe in your own home and relationships so you can focus on supporting your child through trauma therapy.

There are other unique parenting situations that may require some creative planning to build an effective parent-child dyad in therapy. Some kids are cared for by an extended family member or someone who fits the description of kinship care. Other children are raised by foster parents or in group homes. While each of these situations is unique, the answer is remarkably simple: A child simply needs *one* consistent, attuned, highly invested adult who is committed to providing the relational container as the child processes their early memories in therapy. A wide variety of grown-ups can take on this sacred role. In our experience, we have found that adults in this situation report that the process is both intensely emotional and incredibly rewarding.

Supporting the Parent Who Attends Sessions

When one parent is consistently attending sessions, they will often need an opportunity to process what they are personally experiencing in the therapy room. Although every couple will be different, and there is no right way to support each other, here is what we encourage you to share with your co-parent if you are one attending sessions:

- Your feelings about the session and what you need from your partner
- How the session impacted your child

- The key content of the session
- Any new realizations about your child, yourself, or the relationship
- Any new historical information shared by your child
- Ideas for supporting your child today and moving forward
- Any new needs you have to address
- Any new strategies provided by the therapist
- Any to-dos that need to be shared between parents

Although sharing these experiences can be time-consuming and potentially leave you feeling vulnerable, remember that the nonattending parent may feel left out, confused, or unsure of what's happening if they are left in the dark. As a result, they may not know how to effectively respond to the child after sessions, during behavioral episodes, or in moments of intense emotions. We find that the more actively engaged nonattending partners are, the more invested they become in the work that happens between sessions. Nonattending parents play a big role outside of the counseling room in helping their children heal. Since we recognize that many families have busy schedules, we recommend setting aside a specific time to connect with your partner and share whatever information is most important to you after each session. However, depending on the intensity of what you experienced in the therapy room, you may need to change plans and hold off until you have the emotional and physical bandwidth to share your experiences with your partner.

Once you do share this information, know that it is common for the nonattending parent to feel overwhelmed, worried, or concerned about their child. After all, they experience a deep sense of empathy for their child too, so they will need an opportunity to process their feelings as well. Break it down into smaller and more manageable pieces, and be patient with each other. Above all, you want to safeguard your emotional connection with each other so you can stay connected and engaged. Of course, if you are parenting solo, this section is less relevant, but it is still important to share your experiences with another adult, whether a friend or extended family member. They won't need the same level of involvement, and the information you share is meant to help them simply support *you* rather than looking for their contribution to the family system.

Keeping an Eye on Everyone's Health and Wellness

In this chapter, we've talked about the various ways in which the family system can be disrupted when one family member is making significant changes in the way they function. Of course, the goal is for the system to eventually work more effectively, but in the meantime, it is important to address the parts of the system that are in flux. For example, it may fall on the nonattending parent to meet the needs of the other children in the home, both during and after sessions, who may be feeling frustrated, upset, and disappointed. This is why it is so important for both parents to be equally committed to the process of therapy even though only one is attending. Otherwise, it is easy for the nonattending partner to feel resentful about the changing family dynamics rather than taking the lead in supporting their other children.

If you're a solo parent, this may require making adjustments to your routine if you notice that your other children are struggling. How will you know if this is the case? One of the most reliable ways to measure a child's stress is through their baseline functioning in the following areas: eating, sleeping, toileting, social relationships, family relationships, and mood. Knowing your children's baseline in each area is a good place to start. Make a note of this, and if you have any close family members, teachers, or other professionals who regularly observe your children, get their input too. Once you know what is typical for each child, it will be easier to notice changes. For example, a child who typically sleeps through the night but suddenly starts waking up frequently would be showing a change in their baseline behavior.

Alisha and Celeste: Wellness of Other Family Members

Alisha was a single mom who started coming to therapy with her daughter, Celeste, who was just entering kindergarten and showing significant signs of distress. Alisha had been parenting Celeste for the past four years, and although she had some information about her history, there were many unknowns. Within the past year, Celeste's behaviors had escalated and became more confusing and alarming. For example, whenever Alisha would say no to going to the park, Celeste would immediately force herself to have a bowel movement in her underwear and then smear her feces on her mother or on something that her mother liked. Alisha understood that there was a connection between this behavior and Celeste's early trauma, but she was at a loss as to how to make it better. Over time, her patience was wearing thin.

Once they started therapy, they discovered that Celeste's trauma had happened when she was a baby, which meant that Celeste regressed to this developmental age between sessions for most of the time, particularly in the beginning. As a result, Alisha had to revert to early forms of caring for Celeste, such as bottle feeding her, rocking her at night, and helping with all bowel movements. Understandably, this took up quite a bit of her time.

> Celeste's older brother, Jordan, was the only other member of this family. Although he was initially doing well, within the first few weeks of his sister and mom starting therapy, he started to regress in the way he spoke, and his demands for his mother's attention escalated. He began waking nightly, as if he knew that this was the time when Alisha would be the most accessible. At first, Alisha didn't make the connection between Jordan's new behavior and Celeste's trauma therapy.
>
> Later, in a parent-only session, Alisha casually mentioned how tired she was due to these late-night awakenings, and after doing some reflection with the therapist, she came to realize what was happening. In turn, Alisha spent some time talking with Jordan and processing how he was feeling about her time and attention being heavily focused on Celeste. They developed a "secret signal" that Jordan could use to let Alisha know when he was feeling disconnected. Alisha also decided that they might temporarily get more sleep if Jordan slept in her bed. This allowed the system to stabilize and for Alisha to be able to continue the work with Celeste.

Although changes to the family system are inevitable when you start parent-child therapy, some family systems are more flexible than others. When you have a child who has experienced trauma, that flexibility is essential to survival.

CHAPTER 10

Understanding the Process: What Happens in Trauma Therapy

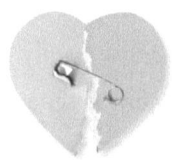

Although we have explored the importance of therapy and explained your role in this process, you may still be wondering what *exactly* your therapist is going to do in session. What strange magic will they impose on you and your child that is going to result in the changes you are hoping for? At the most basic level, trauma therapy will help your child resolve any unpleasant thoughts, feelings, and body sensations that are holding them back, often all in the same session. It will help your child make sense of why the traumatic event occurred, reframe any distorted or negative beliefs they hold about it, and develop a more coherent narrative. How a therapist guides this process will depend on their unique worldview, training, and therapeutic modality. You do not need to be an expert on any of this, but knowing what to expect will make it easier to follow your therapist's lead. With that in mind, let's explore a few concepts that will help you understand what therapists do in session and why they do it.

Therapist Commitment to Attunement

As you learned in chapter 8, attunement involves being aware of and empathically connected to someone's emotional state. When you are attuned to another person, you can sense what is happening inside of them and offer a response that feels on point. Attunement is a crucial quality that all effective therapists must possess, though the specific level of attunement they are able to offer will depend on the nature, length, and openness of the relationship they have with a client. While a highly skilled therapist can develop some basic attunement during their first session with a parent and child, it doesn't compare with the level of attunement that comes from a therapist knowing a family over time. After many sessions and shared experiences, a therapist will begin to recognize the connections between a client's past and present experiences and predict what will feel manageable to them versus what will flood their nervous system. They will be aware of the emotional energy in the room and use this to determine how to move forward.

In parent-child therapy, a therapist must be attuned to multiple different experiences simultaneously, paying attention to both the parent's and child's experiences as well as being in touch with their own. Although the therapist is always attuning to both you and your child, it's probably easier to recognize when they are attuning to your child. They may adjust their body language, tone of voice, and eye contact to be a better match for how your child is presenting. They may use fewer spoken words than you are used to or feel comfortable with. They may ask questions to see, hear, and understand what your child is experiencing on a nonverbal level. For example, if a therapist asks your child, "Can you explain a little more about what happened at school today that was so upsetting?" they are not just looking for facts or information; they are looking at all the different ways your child communicates their experiences. Parents often have the urge to step in if their child isn't answering "properly," isn't answering at all, or is saying things that don't make sense. Check in with yourself if you have these uncomfortable reactions and wait to see how the therapist responds. Therapy is not about compliance or cooperation. It's about understanding one's experience.

Attunement can feel like a slow process, especially if your child presents as withdrawn, dysregulated, or indifferent during therapy. It might seem like your therapist is not doing anything when they allow silence in session or the conversation doesn't seem relevant. In these cases, you might feel tempted to speed things up by jumping in with more information and telling the therapist everything you think they need to know. Before you do this, ask yourself if the therapist needs your input or if this response is a reflection of your own discomfort with not being in control. If you truly feel like the therapist needs some background information about a certain topic, it may be more appropriate to share this information in a parent-only session. We'll discuss the role of silence in sessions later on in this chapter.

Managing the Pace of Sessions

One of the reasons your therapist needs to be attuned to your child's experience is to know when it's time to move forward with the process or slow it down. It is difficult to predict how fast or how intense trauma therapy will be for an individual child. If therapists were to match the speed that parents often wish for, most children would shut down from overwhelm. The therapist's job is to match the child's pace so that this doesn't happen. Since the essence of trauma involves a loss of control, it is essential that we pause and consider the pace that is going to be a good fit for each child: "We cannot emphasize enough how important it is for traumatized children to be given the most possible control, predictability, and ability to moderate the timing, duration, and intensity of their experiences" (Perry & Szalavitz, 2017, p. 313). This is particularly true when we are asking kids to engage in the experience of revisiting trauma memories.

We have lots of tricks up our sleeves to help modulate the speed and intensity of the process. These strategies can be confusing if you aren't familiar with why they are being used. For example, we might move back and forth between asking the child to share a hard story and talking about something funny, as humor can be a valuable tool in mitigating feelings of overwhelm. When we trained to be therapists, we had no idea how valuable our stand-up (or sit-down) comedy skills would be in sessions.

Another way we increase or decrease the intensity of the session is by varying the amount of time we spend processing trauma memories versus practicing regulation skills. In general, we want to have a predictable pattern of how the session time is used, as this makes the experience feel less stressful. Remember that predictability increases feelings of safety. For example, a child may always need to spend some time orienting through play before doing any processing work. However, the amount of time they spend playing will fluctuate depending on whether the focus of that session is memory processing or skill development. Similarly, if a teen is presenting as overwhelmed during session, we shift away from trauma processing to focusing on a current issue or concern that feels safer to discuss and problem solve. In our experience, the biggest struggle with pacing sessions is when the therapist knows the child needs to stay in a "hard place" for a bit longer so change can occur, but everyone else in the room wants to move away from it. Attunement helps the therapist know what your child needs to stay in that hard place and what you need to do to help manage any accompanying hard feelings.

Chapter 10 | *Understanding the Process: What Happens in Trauma Therapy*

Roxie and Mom: Using a Rating Scale to Manage Discomfort

Roxie was a thirteen-year-old girl who attended therapy with her mother but refused to engage or speak during sessions. She would interact with play or art materials when offered but avoided any connection to the trauma. If she perceived any sort of connection between what was happening in the therapy room and her experiences, she would start to get silly, get loud, and regress to childlike behaviors. The therapist was mindful that her tolerance for discomfort was low, yet she carried around an incredible amount of discomfort every day based on her complex trauma.

To increase Roxie's feeling of control in the room, the therapist began implementing a 0–5 rating scale on which Roxie could rate her discomfort. Everyone agreed that Roxie could handle being at a 3 or 4 on the scale for ten minutes, but for the rest of the session she would like to be at a 1 or 2. Over time, Roxie was able to increase from ten minutes to fifteen and eventually to a full thirty minutes when it came to sitting with tough feelings. One of the contributing factors to this gradual move was the increase in her mother's ability to co-regulate with her.

Creating Space for All Behavior in Therapy

We all hold expectations about our own behavior and that of our children, whether these are spoken or unspoken. When you arrive at therapy, you may expect your child to behave a certain way that you consider appropriate. For example, you may expect them to be a willing participant in sessions, answer all questions that are asked of them, and speak in a respectful tone. While we can't speak for all therapists, we generally hold different expectations in counseling than in other settings, like a medical office or school. For example, if you were to take your child to the dentist and they refused to open their mouth, the dentist would not be able to provide the professional service that you came for. If you bring your child to therapy and they refuse to open their mouth, we can work with this! It is for this reason that we created the following "rules of therapy" to help you understand the different expectations we hold for children in counseling.

> ### The Rules of Therapy
>
> It's okay to sit in silence.
>
> It's okay if your child is rude to the therapist.
>
> It's okay if your child refuses to answer a question.
>
> It's okay if your child doesn't sit on the couch properly.
>
> It's okay if they put their feet on the furniture.
>
> It's okay if there's a mess.
>
> It's okay if they accidentally break things.
>
> It's okay if they express angry emotions.
>
> It's okay if they use inappropriate language.
>
> It's okay if they pretend to do something aggressive with the toys.

Chapter 10 | *Understanding the Process: What Happens in Trauma Therapy*

> It's okay if they pretend to ignore what's happening in the room.
>
> It's okay if they resist coming in and it takes time.
>
> It's okay if they have a hard time leaving and need some time.
>
> It's okay if they make noise.
>
> It's okay if they raise their voice.

If your blood pressure spiked while reading this list, check in with the beliefs that are fueling this reaction. This is a great opportunity to ask yourself, *What is stressful about the possibility that my child might behave this way in front of others?* Notice if the feeling you have is embarrassment. Do you worry that it reflects poorly on your parenting abilities? Are you afraid that someone will think negatively of your child? You may also be worried that if you let your child get too wild in the office, you may not be able to bring them back down to baseline, and that's scary.

Therapy is a place where you want your child to be able to demonstrate the full range of emotions they experience. Remember that you have an external regulator in the room—the therapist—who can help you be present with these emotions. It's not all on you when your child gets dysregulated in therapy. That's our job! Trust us, it is highly unlikely that your child is going to do or say something we haven't heard or seen before. The repertoire of shocking behaviors isn't as vast as you might think it is. If you don't act surprised, don't react, and are generally accepting of however your child presents themself in session, they will quickly relax and no longer need to test the boundaries. They will be free to just express themself in whatever way they need to explore the big hurts that brought them to therapy.

Knowing When and How to Contribute

Even when there is a strong parent-therapist alliance in place, some parents find themselves unsure of how and when to contribute to sessions. If you are someone who likes to be in control, it may be difficult to let someone else direct the process, especially when you're not sure whether the focus of therapy should be on your child's current struggles or on the work of healing past hurts. There is no one-size-fits-all answer to this. The reality is that there is a lot of overlap.

For example, let's say you have a parent-child therapy appointment today at 3:00 p.m., and you know the plan is to continue processing your child's early experiences that continue to impact their day-to-day functioning. You are committed to this work. However, today has been a disaster of epic proportions. Your child refused to go to school because their favorite T-shirt wasn't clean. The debate over school or no school led to your child hitting you, along with them making accusations of terrible and untrue things that you have done to make their life hard. As you arrive at the session, you wonder if it's best to move forward with the planned therapy goal or to talk about what happened today. You really want to learn how you and your child can work through these types of days, but you don't want to interrupt the deep work of memory processing.

In this example, neither choice is wrong and both are useful! We recommend talking with your therapist ahead of time to determine how they prefer to handle these situations. Some therapists will ask you to send an email ahead of time, while others will do a quick check-in with you at the office before working with your child. Talking about this issue ahead of time in parent-only sessions will give you clarity and confidence.

Remember that processing trauma memories and making connections between the past and present will naturally resolve the persistent struggles your child has.

Silence is another area that can leave parents feeling uncomfortable or uncertain. As we mentioned earlier, when the therapy room gets quiet, you may have the urge to fill the space with a thought or observation. However, silence serves several important functions in therapy. For example, it:

- Allows time for everyone to process what just happened in session
- Gives time to link this experience to other experiences that are similar
- Allows for the use of (and the noticing of) nonverbal communication
- Offers the child the experience of someone being in the moment with them as they explore their feelings
- Helps everyone in the room resist the urge to fix a problem or spin it positively
- Allows the child to feel attended to and focused on
- Slows down any expectations for more processing

Remember that your child is experiencing an internal battle about revisiting their trauma. Fear has taught them to keep it pushed down, making it feel scary to bring it up. For this reason, it can often feel too intense for them to have a direct conversation about their experiences. In this case, witnessing you and the therapist hold space for them can be easier to tolerate. In the long run, it is far more effective for you to exercise patience and create safety than to push your child to talk. It will also build a more connected parent-child relationship. Pushing your child to do something that is outside of their window of tolerance will only create confusion and disconnection. Your child is battling their own body's fear response. They need you to be on their side so they aren't feeling the need to battle you as well. When you consider how long they have been holding this trauma in their body, it's easier to realize how scary it might feel to them to do something different.

Accessing Simultaneous Parent-Only Consultation

As we mentioned in chapter 3, it is important to do your own inner work before beginning parent-child therapy, but this doesn't mean you can't continue seeking out parent-only sessions throughout the entire process. These consultation sessions are an opportunity for you to better understand your child's reactions to therapy (as well as your own reactions), learn strategies for responding to difficult behaviors in a manageable way, receive advocacy information and other educational resources, learn how to support other family members during therapy, and manage environmental stressors. Of course, how much parent-only support you need will depend on the severity of your child's experiences, how much learning you have done about trauma therapy prior to initiating the process, how your brain processes information, and your financial situation.

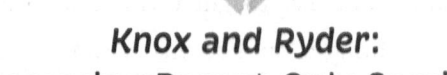

Knox and Ryder: Accessing Parent-Only Sessions

When Knox first began attending therapy with his son, Ryder, he couldn't picture setting up sessions for himself. He believed that the problems existed within his son's behavior and were the result of early experiences that happened to Ryder before Knox started parenting him. Now, three months into therapy, Knox has benefited from these

Chapter 10 | *Understanding the Process: What Happens in Trauma Therapy*

parent-only sessions on more than one occasion. He first booked a session because he wanted to understand more about what was happening to Ryder in sessions and how to manage the new behaviors that were popping up directly after therapy. He was given time to ask questions and feel heard. As Knox learned more about Ryder's trauma and how it impacted his developing brain, he felt increased compassion toward his child. Knox was also able to work through his own emotions about the big behaviors that occurred after session.

Knox returned for additional parent-only sessions after Ryder experienced challenges with a new teacher at school. Knox released his frustrations about not feeling heard by the school, and the therapist provided him with resources and strategies to help him advocate for his son. For example, the therapist recommended that Knox ask the school to rate Ryder's distress on a 5-point scale and to call Knox anytime it moved past a 3. In times of distress, Ryder needed the attunement of his parent to be able to return to his baseline. This also helped preserve the relationships between Ryder and his teacher and classmates by avoiding big meltdowns that often led to aggressive behaviors. The therapist also encouraged Knox to notice when Ryder was struggling to meet expectations at home and school so that Knox could proactively offer more support with activities of daily living than would typically be required.

Knox had grown accustomed to navigating these experiences alone, and it was reassuring to know there was a space for him to go where he would be heard and supported.

As you can imagine, we can't possibly cover everything your therapist might do in a trauma session. However, we hope that we've highlighted some key aspects of the process and common areas of concern so you're feeling more confident while also holding realistic expectations about what trauma therapy will look and feel like. Remember that this will be a growing and learning experience for you as well as your child, and like anything new, it takes time and repetition before it starts to feel more comfortable and familiar.

CHAPTER 11

Preparing for the Commitment of Therapy

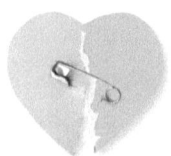

We want your experience with therapy to be successful. In this chapter, we'll discuss several of the common challenges that make it difficult to stay committed to the therapy process, including financial concerns, practical barriers, child resistance, and more. The last thing we want is for you to be dissatisfied with the results of therapy because you encounter obstacles that you weren't prepared for. In these situations, you may find yourself thinking about throwing in the towel. We promise that grappling with these challenges *before* you're in the emotional trenches with your child will make it so much easier to manage. Our greatest desire is for trauma therapy to feel safe, predictable, and manageable for everyone who needs it. Therefore, this chapter will help you notice the signs that you are struggling and give you some strategies for holding on when it gets hard.

Financial Considerations

The expense of trauma therapy can be overwhelming, and the costs don't end with the session fee. There are often other expenses you need to consider, such as taking time off work when necessary, scheduling additional childcare or household support, finding transportation, and (potentially) purchasing equipment required to support your child's ability to self-regulate. Many parents are not prepared for the expense of ongoing therapy, and it can feel frustrating, overwhelming, or even unfair that this will impact other areas of your finances. Indeed, there may be some big decisions your family will need to make about how you allocate your finances. You might be in a position where you will need to put money toward therapy that would otherwise go toward other family expenses, such as vacations, leisure time, dining out, or other nonessential items that the family is used to having.

We aren't saying that counseling should always take priority over other family expenses, as each family situation is unique. Rather, we are encouraging you to be open and honest with your therapist about your budget. It's okay to start therapy with a specific goal in mind, such as targeting one area of trauma without addressing all the traumatic experiences your child has had. Once that goal has been achieved, you can pause and restart therapy when you are able to manage the financial commitment again. This is completely different from going full-steam ahead and suddenly stopping therapy without any warning or planning with your therapist. If this is what you need to do, communicate with your therapist about your financial situation ahead of time so that together you can make a plan that best fits with your finances.

In addition, we have witnessed time and again that some families do not have the insurance benefits needed to access mental health services. Even with extended health benefits, there are often restrictions around the total number of sessions allowed and the specific providers they can see. For example, many families are limited to a total of four sessions or to in-network providers who practice outside of their community, which can prevent them from getting their needs met. If you are experiencing insurance coverage issues, you may need to explore alternative solutions to cover the cost of therapy. For example, you can look into counseling agencies that offer a sliding-scale fee, in which you pay a reduced rate for therapy depending on your income and ability to pay. In addition, we recommend looking through the following ideas to explore any funding resources that might be available to you:

- **Extended health of parents and children:** Your employer may be able to provide your family with extended health benefits that often include counseling services. You will need to check the licensing requirements that your particular insurance provider covers to ensure that the therapist you are choosing has those qualifications.

- **First Nations Health Authority:** This is a government-funded program that provides Indigenous people living in British Columbia with a health benefits plan. Each Canadian province manages the resources provided to Indigenous people differently, although each has a similar program. It covers a certain amount of counseling services with an approved therapist (so ensure your therapist is registered with them). This is an excellent resource for children who have suffered systemic and complex trauma to have ample coverage for ongoing clinical interventions.

- **Online schools:** As part of a well-rounded program for children who are homeschooled, counseling support is often covered for any child whose education is being impacted by mental health or historical trauma concerns. Children are allotted a particular number of sessions they can access during the school year. Families are typically permitted to choose their counselor, provided they are adequately licensed in their province.

- **Postadoption assistance:** When families adopt children from government care, they have the opportunity to apply for post-adoption assistance to meet specific needs of their children. The amount of money they are able to access for counseling will depend on both the needs of their children and their income. This funding must be applied for and is awarded each calendar year or contract term. There appears to be a lack of consistency in how these funds are provided for families across different provinces and communities.

- **Religious organizations:** Many religious organizations have a benevolent fund that they make available for attending families who are experiencing hardship. Counseling is one of the ways that this money is used for families. Decisions about how this money is accessed, how much is available, and who qualifies vary widely among different religions and communities.

- **Disability tax credit:** In Canada, the disability tax credit helps people with disabilities or their supporting family members reduce the amount of income tax they must pay. As a result, families who have children with special needs may receive a tax refund at the end of the year that they can use at their discretion, and some families choose to direct it toward counseling services.

- **Autism funding:** This is a provincial funding source that is available to families of children diagnosed with autism. It provides a predetermined amount of funding, based on the child's age, that can be used for a variety of services, including counseling for the impacted child and their family members.

At the end of the day, it can be difficult to wrap your head around the expense of a process that doesn't guarantee results. If you pay an oral surgeon for a skin graft, you end up with physical evidence of what you paid for. Therapy is a little different. There may be some tangible results you can measure, but when you get them and what they look like are not predictable. While you can't quantify therapy outcomes the same way you can quantify the outcome of a medical procedure, you can use the concepts of *frequency* and *intensity* to notice change. For example, you might notice that the frequency or intensity of your child's meltdowns has decreased over the past month. You might also notice that you're able to understand and communicate with your child better. It might take you a few weeks to start noticing these changes, or it could take a few months, but these changes are occurring.

Pushback and Resistance

As a parent, you may hold certain expectations about how your kid will handle the therapy process. For example, perhaps you believe that they will work hard and cooperate in every session since you are paying for these services. However, what if your child doesn't appear to be interested in therapy at times? Does this mean they don't value or respect the process? Will you feel like they are wasting your time? What you believe about your child's behavior and what you expect cooperation to look like will all contribute to how you feel toward your child.

Take a moment to imagine how "shutdown," "emotional exhaustion," and "anxiety" present in children and how similar that might look to disinterest, disrespect, and defiance. This is an incredible opportunity to shift your interpretation of your child's behavior when they are pushing back on the idea of participating in or even attending therapy. It is a reminder that discomfort, resistance, and exhaustion do not indicate the therapy isn't working. In fact, it's often the opposite. Discomfort, resistance, and exhaustion are responses that our bodies use to fight back when something is shifting and changing. Even when change is good or healthy, our automatic response is to resist it.

When you can recognize your child's pushback as a stress response, you can start by empathizing with your child about what's hard about the process. Try to be as specific as possible regarding what you think is most difficult for your child, and acknowledge that. This might sound like "I'm sorry it's so tiring for you to think about hard things from the past" or "I know this is taking time away from your homework, and you worry about doing well at school." Some children need empathy for engaging in the work of therapy, which they want to do but still find difficult: "I know you think that counseling is helpful, but I can also see that sometimes you wish you didn't have to do it." Remember that trying to logically reason with your child over something they are having an emotional reaction to is likely to be unsuccessful. Notice your own discomfort with their resistance and soothe yourself before supporting them.

Once you have empathized with your child, the next step is to see if there is something practical you can do to ease their discomfort or big feelings. For some children, this means reducing expectations regarding chores and other activities of daily living, while for others it might mean finding a way to make space for what's important to them that counseling is infringing on. Your interest in helping them reduce discomfort is one of the cornerstones of attunement for children with trauma.

The final step is to provide your child with choices that give them some sense of control. For example, you might offer to speak to the therapist about the format of the sessions, remind your child that they are in control of what they say and do in session, and provide them with options for activities you can do before and after each therapy session. In the end, they may still feel resistant and demonstrate this in a variety of ways. Sometimes, you need to make space for resistance rather than try to ignore or change it. This can involve allowing extra time for meltdowns, having extra patience for rude or inappropriate behavior, and making a plan for how you will respond in these situations so you can stay calm. You don't want to increase your child's distress, yet you don't want them to give up on the process. Resistance and pushback can feel tiring for parents, and responding in new ways takes practice. Remember that you are in the process of learning and growing as well. Please extend empathy to yourself in the same way that you do for your child.

James and Audrey: Responding to Pushback

James initially sought out counseling for his daughter, Audrey, because of her extreme dissociative responses. He was concerned with how often she would "space out" and present as detached or emotionally numb. At first, Audrey was making progress as she began processing some of her early traumatic experiences. James was encouraged by the ways she was more present in the moment and more consistent in turning to him when she needed help.

After several sessions of trauma work, James was caught off guard when Audrey started pushing back in big ways. She had never been a kid who was verbally combative, but she had now started yelling and screaming at her dad whenever he asked her to do something she felt she didn't want to do. Even though James knew that challenges could arise in therapy, he was not mentally prepared for this. He was struggling to see how this shift in Audrey's behavior was beneficial. She was clearly overwhelmed, and James was worried that the counseling experience was too much for her. He was also not sure how he was going to manage this behavior if it continued.

> James was close to pulling the plug on their sessions, so he decided to check in with their therapist and share his concerns. The therapist explained that Audrey was finally finding her voice after having been shut down for so long. Together, they were able to come up with a plan that felt supportive for James, which involved empathizing with Audrey about how hard it was to come to session, taking time to prepare before sessions, and introducing a calming, pleasurable activity before and after each session. Feeling heard by the therapist allowed James to find the strength to continue. The family made certain accommodations that allowed for more pushback as Audrey was finding her voice. For example, since Audrey required more time from her dad, they reached out to extended family members who could provide some support in driving the other kids to their after-school activities.

In addition to the expectations you have for your child, you may hold certain beliefs about how other family members will respond to the impact of therapy on daily life, only for them to react another way. Perhaps your spouse didn't realize how much emotional energy this would require and is struggling with the limited energy you have for their needs. Perhaps older siblings who seemed on board in the beginning are now resentful because of the amount of time you are spending with your child attending sessions. Perhaps the family member who is caring for your other children feels like this process is taking too long, and they can't commit to helping forever. These reactions can catch you off guard and make you question your commitment to the process, which is why to the extent possible, it is important to prepare your family ahead of time, as discussed in chapter 9.

However, even with this preparation, not everyone will understand or accept what you are doing and the importance you are placing on it. That's okay! If the people in your life are pushing back, it's important to evaluate whether or not you have the capacity to support them in getting on board. You may need to invest more time and energy in soothing their distress or helping them through their frustration if you really need their assistance to make parent-child therapy happen. You may also need to briefly pause therapy (refer back to chapter 9) and put your energy into solidifying your family system before you can move forward. If you are able to find alternative supports, you may even choose to distance yourself from any unsupportive family members while you are in the process of trauma therapy.

Strategies for Holding On When You Have the Urge to Quit

We have witnessed many families who have become overwhelmed by the ripple effects that therapy can have on the family system, leading them to want to discontinue counseling. Perhaps this has been your experience as well. If you've arrived at a place where you are thinking, *That's it. I'm done. It's time to quit*, then you might want to bookmark this page for future reference. We have all been in emotionally charged situations where it's hard to think clearly. The first step is always to take some time to get regulated. You can't make any good decisions in an emotionally charged state. Stay hydrated, go for a walk, get some sleep, and deep breathe over the next twenty-four hours before making any big decisions; even better, try to spend a few minutes doing an activity that brings you joy. We find that this can shift your thinking and remind you that there are still ways you can feel good.

Next, talk through the decision with a trusted person. In the end, you probably know what the right answer is, but you may need someone to sit beside you while you sort it out. It's extra helpful if this person has some experience with parenting a child with trauma or is familiar with the process of therapy. Sit with your own experience for a bit until you can identify what triggered your recent urge to quit. Sometimes, a child's experience of exhaustion, hopelessness, or frustration will transfer over to us as parents—and this may be the case for you too. Did something happen in a recent session that touched on your own experiences? If so, you may have the sudden feeling of wanting to get as far away from those feelings as possible. We encourage you to discuss these concerns with your therapist, as they will have some ideas to help with these overwhelming feelings. They can also walk you through your options, such as taking a short break, and discuss how each option may impact the process. Therapists understand real life. We want to set you up for success.

Finally, look through the following strategies, which can provide you with much-needed support and give you the motivation to stick it out when things get hard:

- Ask for help with daily tasks. You will feel so much better if you don't have to make dinner tonight or drive your kids to their third soccer practice this week.

- Spend quality time with people who lift you up. You deserve to feel good, and trusting relationships can offer this.

- Write about your experiences in a journal (or leave yourself a voice note about these experiences). Getting your feelings out can help you get to the root of what is causing your distress or discomfort.

- Take advantage of the option to have parent-only sessions. This can meet your needs and give you the energy or courage to continue.

- Pay attention to the way you talk to yourself. Oftentimes, we put ourselves down with self-defeating statements like "I can't do this" or "Things will never get better." In contrast, when we speak to ourselves with gratitude and appreciation, we have more energy and motivation to do hard things.

- Remind yourself of why you are doing this. Knowing the *why* helps you stay the course when things get hard.

- Ask for feedback from others who see the progress you are making. Other people may see changes over time that you don't notice.

- Increase the number of pleasurable experiences you engage in with your child (and other children). Think about what makes both of you smile or laugh.

- Look for someone new whom you haven't already asked for support. There may be someone in your life who would feel honored to help.

What Happens When You Stop Too Soon

Going to trauma therapy is a bit like opening an old wound. Just like you wouldn't leave the hospital with only half of the necessary stitches in place, you don't want to leave your child with their emotional wounds exposed to the elements without protection. One of the risks of ending therapy suddenly and prematurely is that your child may perceive it to be their fault. They may worry that it's taking them too long to get better or that they aren't working hard enough. If they exhibited big behaviors during or after sessions, they might assume their behavior was too much for the therapist or you to handle. Another risk of ending therapy too soon is that it causes the child to lose their relationship with the therapist, which reinforces their belief that the people close to them will eventually leave or abandon them. Without a proper explanation, kids will always fill in the blanks for themselves, and the stories they create are often self-deprecating.

In addition, certain types of trauma, such as sexual abuse or ritualistic abuse, may have a bigger impact on the brain and body if left unprocessed. That's because there is often more shame involved due to the way society views these types of experiences. For example, sexual abuse survivors often feel confused about consent and blame, and the dissociation that often accompanies this type of abuse has the capacity to change the way the brain develops. As a result, kids may continue to relive these traumatic memories more intensely or more frequently than before, or they may lock these memories down in a way that will make them hard to access again later.

Although parents never intentionally want to put their child in this position, certain life circumstances and competing demands can lead to a sudden and unexpected end to trauma therapy. When this occurs, themes of the child's unprocessed trauma can show up in daily life, either immediately after sessions stop or a few months later. This is the brain and body's way of doing the work without the support of therapy. We've seen it happen countless times, so it only seems right to give you a heads-up on what might happen and what you can do about it. In these situations, it will be important to respect your child's need to process difficult memories without therapy and to support them in a practical way as best you can during this time. You can do so by reducing expectations of daily living, offering sensory-based tools and comfort items, providing reminders of what is safe, and responding with attunement.

Paris and Jake: Closing Memories for Now

Paris was a busy parent of multiple children with intense needs. She started therapy with her oldest son, Jake, to help him process his significant early childhood traumas. Jake was regularly attending sessions and growing his self-confidence, which was so wonderful for Paris to see. However, whenever he was scared, he continued to struggle with punching, throwing things, and threatening physical harm to himself or others. Paris had a good understanding of where Jake's behaviors were coming from, but it was nonetheless causing a lot of harm to the family, especially as Jake continued to get older and stronger.

During one of Jake's daily outbursts, Paris decided to cancel their next therapy session until things calmed down a bit. Her intention was to rebook the session, but she was so overwhelmed by everything that was happening around her that she continued to let it slip her mind. At first, Jake's behavior calmed down for a few weeks, but then it began to escalate again. Jake continued to work through the traumatic experiences he was having in therapy by himself.

Paris's exhaustion was making it hard for her to imagine continuing with therapy. She consulted with their therapist, who suggested a shift away from trauma therapy to sessions that would focus more on regulating Jake's sensory experiences and developing tools to manage the big behaviors at home. Before they made this shift, the therapist walked Paris and Jake through the process of "closing a memory" so he wouldn't continue to be triggered by it. Paris also took the time to reflect on where she was and how she was struggling with the competing demands of her other children's needs.

Pausing trauma therapy while they continued with regular counseling sessions gave Paris the space to restructure things so she could manage Jake's trauma therapy sessions when they felt ready to start back up again.

In addition, we encourage parents to allow their child enough time to hear and process the story of why they won't be going back to therapy, either now or ever. Creating a story of what happened—and why—will help the child understand and internalize this narrative rather than allowing them to create a negative story about themself. Stories that explain difficult concepts with a past, present, and future lens help children organize their thoughts and process their feelings, especially when these stories are repeated many times. We encourage you to include images in the story to pique your child's interest and improve their ability to absorb the information. The story serves as a reminder of why they went to therapy, what happened while they were there, why the therapy stopped, who will help with their big feelings now, and what the plan for the future is.

CHAPTER 12

Managing Your Own Reactions in Session

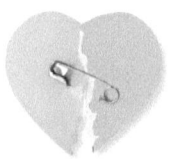

So, you've finally made the leap, and you are attending sessions with your child. Congratulations! You have had to overcome a bunch of mental hurdles and emotional landmines to get here, but you believe in what you are doing. You have also developed a strong relationship with your therapist and trust that they know what they are doing. Although you may have assumed that the biggest obstacles would be behind you at this point, now that you are attending sessions, you realize that the process doesn't feel good. Your child might be saying things about you that hurt deeply. You might be watching them grapple with intense feelings in session and feel guilty that you can't take the pain away. You might be seeing a different set of reactions in the therapy room from when you are at home, and it's leaving you unsure of what to do or say. They might be rejecting your efforts to comfort or soothe them. Rejection is painful as it is, but when it comes from your child, it seems to have an even bigger sting.

The following is a list of reactions that children and teens frequently have in trauma therapy that can cause you to feel uncomfortable. Knowing that these reactions are common when children are working through big hurts will help you feel less surprised and overwhelmed if you encounter them:

- Saying no to any offers of comfort
- Yelling and screaming
- Physically moving away from you
- Dissociating or numbing out
- Insulting you or calling you names
- Lying or accusing you of things you didn't do
- Pushing your triggers
- Hiding or covering themselves
- Ignoring or not responding to you
- Turning to the therapist for comfort
- Asking for the comfort of someone not present
- Saying or doing things to embarrass you
- Saying or doing things to control you

Let's walk through a common reaction that has the potential to be disruptive. It becomes apparent in session that your child has lied to you about something. You instantly notice an increase in body temperature, particularly in your neck and chest, your heart rate increases, and you seem to be consumed with anger. Because you've done your own preparation work, you know how to name what you are feeling ("I am feeling myself have a big reaction and I know this is my body's way of telling me this is painful") and spend a few minutes taking some deep breaths and squeezing a stress ball. Your therapist is also aware of this plan and reminds you to drink some water from your water bottle. As you do so, your therapist narrates for your child what is happening as a healthy example of how we notice and attend to our feelings.

If you find yourself in the middle of one of these experiences, remember to stay calm and confident so you can continue showing up amid the discomfort. If you are having difficulty doing so, it's okay to take a short break to work on whatever is triggering you. This can look like asking your therapist to pause while you take some deep breaths and drink some water. Or if you need to leave the room, it can look like asking for a bathroom break to have a minute to attend to yourself. The important thing about breaks is that they are presented as a way to meet your need in the moment, not a reaction to what your child said or did. Even if you have done your own inner work and prepared yourself in advance as best you can, it can still be hard to predict how you will respond in a situation that strikes a nerve. In these situations, your brain and body may react in ways that are surprising even to you. For example, you may find yourself:

- Smiling or laughing from embarrassment or discomfort
- Ignoring the behavior as though it didn't happen
- Shutting down and disengaging from the conversation
- Defending yourself with various arguments
- Accusing your child of lying or not participating appropriately
- Feeling an urgency to leave
- Thinking about quitting therapy
- Looking to the therapist for support or comfort
- Threatening a consequence, either verbally or with a facial expression

When you are in session, you might feel like you need to suppress those reactions because you are in the presence of someone else. However, as we discussed in chapter 7, your child is likely to pick up on this discrepancy—not to mention that children and teens are happy to call you out when your responses don't feel authentic or genuine. Instead, it's important to be honest about how you are feeling so you can work through any potential roadblocks with your therapist. Maybe you need some extra parent-only sessions to work through your discomfort or agitation. Maybe you need more support in managing your child's behaviors at home so your frustration does not spill over in session. Whatever it is, learning how to manage your own reactions to your child's emotions—and building tolerance to these experiences—is key.

Grant and Mei: Managing Reactions to a Child's Emotions in Session

Grant started therapy with his daughter, Mei, with some confidence since he'd gone through his own experience of trauma therapy. He could make sense of Mei's hurt and understood why she expressed such big emotions when she was triggered. At home, he would use relaxation and distraction techniques to help her shift out of these big feelings whenever they arose. For example, he would turn on her favorite music, bring her a special snack, or allow her time on her iPad. Grant was comfortable helping Mei manage her emotions using this strategy.

When they began counseling and Mei was asked to recall some difficult experiences, Grant found it incredibly challenging to sit with Mei's discomfort and not try to shift her out of her feelings. He noticed that he could tolerate her distress for a few minutes, but he then became agitated and struggled to keep his focus on Mei. Sitting with her in her distress for longer than a few minutes felt wrong. He felt like he wasn't helping her and that he was leaving her in her pain.

> Grant noticed that it was hard for him to take the therapist's lead at this point, as he was experiencing a conflict between what his brain knew he should do and what his body was begging him to do. On a cognitive level, he knew that allowing Mei to feel her feelings was part of the process, but on an emotional level, he wanted to make her pain stop.
>
> Grant felt anger building up inside because he couldn't act in the way that he felt was best for his child in that moment. He didn't feel able to sit in Mei's pain any longer. Since Grant was accustomed to the experience of trauma therapy, he was genuinely surprised that these feelings were surfacing for him during his daughter's session, so he took some time with the therapist to process what was going on for him and to develop some skills he could use in future sessions to increase his ability to tolerate her discomfort.

When New Information Comes Up

A therapist's skill and ability to ask about your child's experiences may lead them to share stories you have never heard them speak of before, either because of their developmental level or their desire to keep big feelings at bay. Be open to the idea that the narrative you have may not fit with how your child remembers events from their past. They may have a gut feeling about what happened to them that only emerges when someone asks questions that allow them to access the emotional content of those memories. For example, a therapist might ask a child what they think they were like as a baby, and the child automatically responds with negative statements, such as "I was ugly," "I cried too much," or "I was needy." Further exploration typically reveals that the child believes these negative attributes were the cause of any rejection or abandonment they experienced.

These new memories may emerge for a variety of reasons. First, some children may not have had a chance to explore specific events that occurred in their lives, such as separation from parents, hospitalizations, or traumas related to typical daily experiences (like riding in a car or sitting at a dinner table). A therapist's specific training allows them to guide conversations that help children explore and articulate what they remember and feel about these experiences. Second, some children have traumatic memories that haven't been processed, such as a child who was removed from their birth parents at the age of four. This specific memory can be accessed through therapy to help the child experience the memory from a place of safety and control. Third, during trauma processing, other memories may be uncovered, given that the brain links together experiences that activate similar feelings in our bodies, causing a chain reaction where one memory leads to others. Trauma triggers may also be activated outside of session, and the child then brings that experience with them the next time they see their therapist.

When you hear stories in the therapy office that you didn't know about before, it can create feelings of anxiety about whether you can trust your child to be open and honest with you. You may also worry about your ability to provide effective supervision or support. We want to reassure you that it is typical for your child to reveal new information in session, as the therapy room is a safe place where they can explore their emotions and experiences. It is also normal for many children to only open up about these memories in session. This is an innate protective response to ensure that they are in a safe place when releasing intense emotional material.

As you become more familiar with how memories work and the ways in which they need to be expressed, you can learn to become a safe place for future disclosures. To create the type of safety required for your child to explore their memories, you need to be aware of your own reactions and to remember that your child needs you to show up as an attuned, caring presence in these moments. You need to create a safe place by not becoming overwhelmed by the content of the memory and by showing your child that you are confident in your ability to help them get back to a place of regulation. In addition, safety means that you always believe your child's memories even when they don't seem realistic. Finally, you need to allow your child to be in control of how much, with whom, and where something is shared. For example, they may only want to share a memory with one parent, and safety means that they get to choose that.

When Your Trauma Gets Triggered During Session

If you have a history of traumatic experiences, and you notice these memories getting activated in session, it is important to let your therapist know right away. Memories, whether repressed or dormant, can impact how you respond to your child—both in session and in your daily interactions with them. Remember that your own lived experiences are also in the therapy room, so certain words, feelings, and sensations can trigger something in you and bring you back to an earlier experience you had forgotten about. It's incredible how parenting causes us to revisit our earlier experiences. You may even find yourself triggered by something you didn't anticipate or don't understand. If you feel confused or uncertain about a trigger and where it came from, or you continue to feel activated long after leaving the session, this is an indication that a parent-only session with your therapist would be beneficial.

Carla and Jordan: Unexpected Parent Trigger in Session

Carla brought her eight-year-old son, Jordan, in for therapy to address the significant aggression she was experiencing from him at home. Although she had developed healthy coping strategies to manage this behavior, she was hoping therapy would help them get to the bottom of where this aggression was coming from. During their third parent-child session, Jordan became dysregulated when his carefully built block structure came tumbling down unexpectedly. Carla offered an appropriate level of empathy, to which Jordan responded by abruptly standing up and yanking out a handful of Carla's hair. Carla instinctually responded by cowering and crying, her tone shifting and sounding like a small child.

The therapist recognized this dramatic change in Carla's presentation and the way in which she was looking to the therapist to save her. To help Carla pull herself out of the trauma trigger, the therapist suggested that she stand up. As Carla stood, Jordan was no longer able to reach his mom's head and stopped trying to pull her hair. Carla also experienced a shift when she was no longer on the floor with someone standing over her and hurting her. She quickly regained her composure and was able to see the situation from her adult perspective.

Once Carla was feeling in control of her body again, she was able to focus on Jordan and help him get back to a state of calm. At the end of the session, the therapist encouraged Carla to reach out to set up a parent-only session to help her explore what was clearly a significant trigger. As they worked together one-on-one, Carla was able to recall other moments at home when she had also felt triggered but had attributed

> it to managing a child with aggressive behaviors. With the support of her therapist, Carla was able to explore experiences of abuse that she had experienced in her family of origin. Carla shared with her therapist an appreciation for being able to work through this while her child was still young. She could only imagine how difficult this would have been to deal with when her child was in a bigger body.

Whenever you find yourself getting triggered in session—whether due to known or repressed memories—we recommend walking yourself through the following self-reflection questions, either with your therapist or on your own. These questions will help you observe, notice, and process the experience you had in session. You might recognize some of these questions from chapter 7, when we provided you with a journaling template to process your feelings from a session. Start by thinking of a moment in the session when you felt your emotions intensify or you felt like your reaction (either internal or external) was out of proportion with what was happening in the moment. Then ask yourself what sensations, emotions, and thoughts you were having, seeing if you can connect these experiences to an earlier time in your life.

Once you have made this connection, think about what you wish you could have done (or what someone else could have done) differently to help you through this upsetting experience. Are there certain words you wish you had said or actions you wish you had taken at the time to protect yourself? Use this as an opportunity to resolve that prior experience and shift the trigger from being stuck to being integrated into your memories. You might replay it in your mind with a different ending that allows you to use the current capacity of your voice and body to protect yourself. Or you might replay the memory and include a protective figure who is able to help you end or escape the experience. For example, if you were in an abusive situation as a child from which you could not run away or leave, you might wish that you could have fought back or that someone would have stopped the abuse. In this case, you can give yourself an opportunity to integrate that experience by moving your body in a way that helps you find release, such as leaving the room or asking for help.

> ### Parent Post-Session Reflection Questions
>
> → **Sensations:** What did it feel like in your body?
>
> Example: *I felt my face get hot and my throat close, and it seemed like I couldn't get any words out.*
>
> → **Emotions:** What emotions did you experience?
>
> Example: *I felt embarrassed and guilty, like I had done something wrong and someone would find out.*
>
> → **Thoughts:** What were you thinking?
>
> Example: *I was worried the therapist was going to think that I'm a terrible parent because I am now realizing that I responded in emotionally harmful ways to my child in the past.*
>
> → When was another time in your life when you might have had a similar feeling or reaction?
>
> Example: *I've felt this feeling before when I was younger and really scared that my parents would find out things that I had done that they didn't approve of. I was always so scared of what they would say and do. I don't think they would have hurt me, but I know that the shame of them knowing would have been unbearable.*
>
> → What do you wish you could have done differently at that time? Express what you wanted to do or say in the moment by talking about it, writing about it, or engaging in a physical action.

> **Example:** I wish I could have felt safe and bold enough to say what was happening to me. I wanted to express how I felt about my experiences to my parents without feeling so scared that they would see me differently, reject me, or make me feel like there was something wrong with me. I wanted someone to help me get out of the mess I was in. As a parent myself now, I need to be able to ask for help without feeling ashamed. I need to be able to be honest about my current experiences so that I don't keep them bottled up inside until I explode. It would feel so good to share with someone that I feel like I've failed my kids and done things that I am not proud of and know that they aren't going to reject me.

If this is difficult in the beginning, you may need some support from a therapist until it starts to feel safe and familiar. As time goes on, you may find that you don't need to be as intentional about answering these questions because it will become a natural process you do whenever you feel something come up for you.

CHAPTER 13

Noticing Your Child's Overwhelm

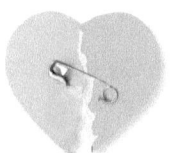

There may be times during trauma therapy when your child starts to get overwhelmed. This can manifest as excessive tiredness, withdrawal, refusal to attend sessions, and unforeseen anger toward yourself or the therapist. It can also manifest as regression, in which your child is suddenly unable to do things for themselves, constantly needs to be in physical contact with you, or forgets how to do regular daily tasks. When children are overwhelmed, it can be difficult for them to put their experience into words and ask for what they need. They likely don't understand what's happening inside of them or what would make it better.

In these situations, paying attention to their physical, relational, behavioral, and emotional cues will give you the information you need. For example, your child might suddenly refuse to go to sleep alone after doing this successfully for years, or they might forget new math concepts they've learned when they typically have a good memory. Here are some behaviors to watch for when you suspect your child is feeling overwhelmed.

Physical	- Difficulty sleeping - Changes in appetite - Increased food intolerances - Digestive issues - Changes in energy levels (e.g., lethargy) - Unexplained aches and pains - Changes in sensory sensitivities - Stomachaches or headaches - Frequent injuries and illnesses - Temporary loss of memories
Relational	- Alternating between pulling close (clinginess) and pushing away (rejection) - Projecting their feelings or emotions on others - Peer conflict or rejection - Defiance or overcompliance - Excessive desire for independence - Longing for someone who has harmed them
Behavioral	- Explosive behaviors - Self-harm - Physical aggression or desire to harm others - Perfectionism - Obsessive-compulsive behaviors - People-pleasing - Hoarding - Risk-taking behaviors - Increased hypervigilance
Emotional	- Mood swings - Protracted low mood or sadness - Manic symptoms (e.g., increased agitation, energy) - Frequent crying or screaming - Excessive or increased anxiety - Perceived helplessness - Panic - Spacing out

We often hear from parents who struggle to know whether the regression they are noticing is related to what's happening in therapy or to another factor in the child's life. This can be tough to tease apart. For example, you may have a child who is processing a memory related to rejection or loss in their early years, while they are simultaneously struggling with peers at school and experiencing similar themes of rejection in those relationships. In this example, it may not be one situation or the other that is triggering the regression; it could be both.

The important point is that when you notice a change in your child's baseline functioning that lasts more than a few days, we encourage you to pay attention regardless of where it seems to be coming from. We also encourage you to notice whether your child is having any out-of-proportion (or as the kids often say, "out-of-pocket") reactions to typical childhood or adolescent stressors, which indicate that there might be more happening below the surface. For example, your child might demonstrate an out-of-proportion reaction if their sibling lightly brushes up against them and they react by screaming and crying as if they are in severe physical pain.

Jasmine and Ada:
An Out-of-Proportion Reaction

Jasmine came home from school one day and told her mom, Ada, that someone on the playground had slapped her across the face. Ada empathized with how scary and upsetting this would be and suggested they talk to the teacher the next day. After speaking with the teacher—who was confused and recalled that Jasmine was the one having struggles with peers and appeared down the day before—Ada got the impression that the incident may not have happened the way Jasmine reported it.

> Ada took a few hours to process her own feelings about the idea that her daughter may have lied to her. In Ada's upbringing, lying to a parent was not tolerated, and giving consequences for this behavior would have become the focus of the situation. However, Ada took some time to consider that the peer conflicts Jasmine was experiencing were connected to what she was processing in therapy. After some time, Ada went back to Jasmine and empathized with the friendship struggles that she had not realized her daughter was experiencing on the playground. The empathy that Jasmine received from her mother allowed Jasmine to admit that while she had not been slapped, the way her friends had treated her hurt a lot.

You'll want to give the other adults in your child's life a heads-up about these out-of-proportion reactions as well. Your child's grandparent, for example, might find it easier to respond to a huge outburst if they understand that it is connected to something deeper your child is working through. Otherwise, they might respond to the child with statements like "Why are you making such a big deal of this?" or "You don't get to act this way just because you are having a hard time" or "Why are you acting this way? There is no reason for it." When grown-ups respond with statements such as these, the child moves into a place of shame, which can lead them to further withdraw or lash out. However, when grown-ups realize where the child's response is coming from, they are more likely to respond with compassion and understanding, which protects against shame and disconnection.

Chapter 13 | *Noticing Your Child's Overwhelm*

Recognizing the Overwhelm in Day-to-Day Life

When you are feeling overwhelmed, your normal family or work expectations can feel like too much. As a result, maybe you feed your entire family cereal for dinner one night because cooking something feels impossible that day. Or perhaps you spontaneously institute pajama Friday in your house because there aren't enough clean clothes in anyone's drawers and the thought of doing laundry is overwhelming. These are ways you temporarily reduce the intensity of your physical or emotional load until you can find the energy to recover. The next day, you resume your regular meals and have some clean clothes ready for the kids.

So, what about when your child experiences overwhelm? What are they able to skip out on or leave until later? Do they have the option of postponing chores, skipping homework for the day, or spending the weekend in a messy bedroom? Without realizing it, you might be requiring your kid to continue their routine even though they don't have the bandwidth for it. After all, trauma therapy requires an incredible amount of physical and emotional energy. Your child is spending time in session processing trauma triggers, learning new regulation skills, and changing ingrained patterns of behavior—all of which require them to form new pathways in their brain. The process of creating new neural pathways is akin to the experience of riding your bike every day through the same field of grass. Over time, the grass wears away until the dirt is visible. And after even more time, your tires will eventually leave a groove in the ground that will make riding so much easier. This easier route will become your preferred route, and it's unlikely you'll think about going in a different direction to reach your destination. Why would you? This way is easier.

It's the same thing when you are trying to teach your child new ways of responding as they heal their traumas: You are asking them to form new pathways. You are asking them to *not* choose the ready-made path and to engage in the hard work of creating a new pathway. This is difficult work, as the brain wants to resist and do what feels familiar, even if it isn't good or helpful anymore. By using this analogy, you can remind yourself that it is a process and celebrate the seemingly small but significant steps your child takes forward. The path in their brain that wants to avoid any big feelings associated with trauma is well worn and easier to travel. Creating new pathways in the brain takes hard work and repetition!

When you're able to notice the energy your child is putting into counseling—and you demonstrate this knowing by lightening their load in whatever way you can—it helps your child feel connected to you. For example, if your child struggles with feeding themself at dinner, you might offer to help feed them. If your child struggles with falling asleep, you might increase the amount of time you spend lying in bed next to them so they can drift off peacefully. If your child struggles with completing homework or keeping their room organized, you might step in and support them in these tasks. Keep in mind that reducing the load is only helpful if your child perceives it to be so. If you remove something from your child's schedule that they find regulating or that brings them joy, this won't be helpful. For example, for one child, the option to stay home from soccer practice after an exhausting therapy session might feel like a relief, while for another child, it would seem like punishment because moving their body and connecting with peers feels good. You know your child best. With some observation and reflection, you will find the right ways to temporarily lighten the load.

Noticing When Overwhelm Impacts School

As we discussed earlier, when children have experienced trauma, their bodies are in a constant state of hypervigilance, as they scan their environment for any potential threats. Not surprisingly, this can interfere with a child's ability to learn, grow, and meet expectations at school. Even once kids start trauma therapy, the emotional and physical energy that they must direct into trauma processing leaves little energy for anything else. As a result, many kids find themselves struggling even more at school, or in different ways, than they were before.

For example, kids may appear to be engaging in classroom activities but later indicate they have no memory of anything they were taught. They may also experience a temporary loss of skills that they had previously learned, such as forgetting the foundational skills of long division, even though previous mastery had been evident. Or they may struggle to find the words to articulate themselves, which can negatively impact their verbal or written responses to classroom activities. Many children in trauma therapy simply don't have the stamina for a full day of school, cannot sustain concentration, and find it difficult to meet homework expectations.

We find that planning ahead with your child's school can go a long way in preventing misunderstandings and unrealistic expectations when your child is struggling. Be an advocate for your child by explaining to school staff why you will be prioritizing trauma therapy over school participation. This is easier to orchestrate for children in primary school versus adolescents, who have more complex demands on their schedule, so this should be done with a great deal of care and consideration. We recommend offering a simple explanation like the following to open communication and increase the flexibility of school staff:

> *My child is going to be engaging in trauma therapy, and as a parent, I feel this is going to be a demanding experience for them. I am choosing to prioritize therapy over all other aspects of my child's development because I've noticed that their early childhood experiences are impacting their ability to be successful at school, in relationships, and in pursuing their own interests. This is consistent with the research I've done on the importance of resolving trauma while children are still young. This means that at times, my child will miss school, be unable to prioritize homework, and need additional accommodations to stay regulated at school. To help me assess how my child is managing this process, I would really appreciate your support in noticing the following behaviors: [state the target behaviors you have identified in therapy]. You can communicate your observations by email or phone. Please let me know at any time if you have questions or concerns. I want to work collaboratively with you.*

At the same time, your child may show improvements in certain skill areas because of therapy. For example, they may learn how to better articulate their feelings, allowing them to share any fear, sadness, disappointment, or rejection that they are experiencing at school. While this reflects amazing progress, it can also be a challenge. For example, let's say your child is in elementary school, and they go through the routine experience of moving from one classroom to another, like going from music to the library. With each classroom change, the adult in charge changes. Although your child has gone along with this routine for years, they now start reporting these experiences as "scary" and struggle during these transitions. Since your child has never shown fear in this context before, teachers might be inclined to look for another explanation, such as noncompliance or defiance. However, the reality is that these classroom transitions can be a scary experience for a child whose upbringing included multiple caregivers and moves. Without this awareness, school staff will miss out on opportunities to validate, soothe, and connect with your child. You are your child's best advocate. Preparing the adults who support your child will empower them to meet needs they would otherwise overlook or be unaware of.

Rituals and Routines to Reduce Overwhelm

Consistent rituals and routines can help your child manage any overwhelming feelings they experience both in and around therapy sessions. Remember, predictability helps kids feel safe. When they trust that there aren't going to be any big surprises, their body doesn't need to be on high alert. You don't want them to feel like therapy is another scary experience they need to be watching out for, so consider what rituals you can wrap around this experience for them. It might be stopping for a snack at the same place each time you travel to the therapy office. It might be going for a walk or visiting a park for playtime on the way home after session. Here is a list of ideas you can try, either before or after sessions.

Ideas for Routines and Rituals to Create Predictability

→ Do a preferred activity (e.g., going to a playground, cuddling with the dog, kicking a soccer ball).
→ Have quiet time with no talking.
→ Have alone time with a parent.
→ Listen to music or audiobooks.

- → Stop somewhere for a snack, meal, or drink.
- → Do a sensory activity (e.g., spinning on a chair, holding a weighted toy, chewing gum).
- → Tell funny stories or jokes.
- → Remember highlights from the week.
- → Read a book.
- → Draw or engage in another creative arts activity.
- → Drive a particular route to and from the session.
- → Look at comforting pictures.
- → Sing along to favorite songs or loud music on the drive.
- → Play a game (e.g., I spy, clapping games, card games).
- → Nap on the way home.

Don't be afraid to try out a few ideas or come up with your own as well. You know your child or teen best and can anticipate what would feel good for them. Notice what their body needs and what helps them feel most regulated. There is no right way to build in rituals or routines, as long as it feels good for your child. Bonus points if it also feels good for you.

Taking Breaks and Managing Priorities

Other life events may emerge while you are in trauma therapy that create unexpected overwhelm for you, your child, or the whole family. This can include crises (such as an illness or death in the family) or positive life events that require more time, energy, or resources (such as your child's sports team making the playoffs or having extended family come from overseas to stay for the summer). These are a few real-life examples that have caused some of the families we've worked with to put trauma therapy on pause:

- Surgery or other medical intervention for a family member
- A new opportunity for the child or family member
- A death in the family or a significant illness of a family member
- Summer break or family vacations
- The urgency of other therapies or interventions, such as occupational or physical therapy
- Another child in the family who is in crisis
- A heavy academic semester at school
- A significant financial issue or loss of extended health benefits

When life events such as these happen, it may mean that trauma therapy needs to be put on hold until there is enough time and space for sessions and everyone is ready to reengage. There are a few different ways to accomplish this. One option is to continue therapy but shift to a different treatment modality that does not activate trauma memories. Another option is to reduce the frequency of sessions or move to online sessions to reduce the time commitment that driving requires. With these options, the therapeutic work continues in some way, but the processing of trauma events is temporarily paused.

If the whole family needs to take a break from trauma therapy for an extended period, everyone will benefit from some preparation. Some children move right through this experience without missing a beat (they may even seem happy about the break), while others struggle significantly. They may experience anxiety about potential loss, not just of the therapist but of the experience they've created with you in session. Although they may not be able to verbalize what this feels like, they are losing the opportunity to have a predictable time and space to share with someone who is focused only on them.

We also want to caution you that it is easy to misinterpret any seemingly positive reactions your child might have to pausing therapy. For example, when the intensity of trauma therapy is reduced, they may seem more relaxed and less in need of your attention or connection. This might lead you to believe that they have resolved the stories of their past and that there is no need to continue therapy in the future. However, it is likely that your child has other memories or experiences that they haven't had the opportunity to process yet. Sometimes, taking a break from activating memories can give the illusion that they are resolved.

Deanna and Eli: Planning a Break from Trauma Therapy

Deanna and her son, Eli, had been attending trauma counseling for eight months. Eli had made tremendous progress so far in working through several trauma triggers, and he was currently working hard to process his earliest experiences with food insecurity. At the same time, Deanna's youngest child was struggling with many different physical health symptoms, but the doctors had not been able to narrow down what was causing them. This process of going to the doctor, being referred to a specialist, and waiting for the appointments had been going on for over a year.

Just this week, Deanna was alerted by one of the specialists that her daughter had a life-threatening illness that required immediate treatment. The treatment would begin with surgery but would then require several weeks of recovery at the hospital, followed by six more months of ongoing treatment appointments. On top of the devastation Deanna was feeling,

> she knew that she would not be able to continue with Eli's trauma therapy sessions. She knew the unexpectedness of this sudden change would be hard for Eli to manage, on top of all the feelings he would experience when hearing the news about his sister's health.
>
> Deanna met with the counselor to develop a plan that would help Eli feel supported even though he wouldn't be continuing trauma therapy at this point. They planned for Deanna to offer Eli scheduled one-on-one time throughout the week to allow him to feel seen and heard. They also rehearsed specific strategies Deanna could use to support Eli with his worries regarding food. In the next parent-child session, they discussed the reason for these changes and how Eli would continue to receive help from his family. Through their discussion, Deanna felt that ongoing parent-consultation sessions would be beneficial even though they could not continue with parent-child therapy at this time. Deanna was also able to schedule a final session for Eli to allow for some closure for him at this time.

Finally, when a child has resolved their early complex memories, it may be time to end regular therapy. For example, when a child has reached a place where their triggers are reduced, their regulation is improved, and they can tell a coherent story about what happened to them, these are all signs that it may be a good time to close therapy—at least for now. However, a "resolution" of a trigger at one developmental stage does not mean that it will not resurface at a different developmental stage. Indeed, in our experience of providing trauma therapy to people spanning ages two to seventy-two, we've discovered that a resolution in the present moment can shift when a new life stage begins. This doesn't mean that a person must reprocess everything that has happened to them. What they need is an opportunity to reflect on their past experiences with a new level of understanding and insight. It's akin to a system update that becomes available on our digital devices every so often. We don't need to reprogram the entire device; we just need to install the updated version. Just as our understanding of the world grows and changes with age, so does our understanding of the traumas we have experienced. This may create more uncomfortable feelings in the present until we can resolve our new awareness and integrate them into our new worldview.

Reconciling the Urge to Protect and the Need to Heal

At this point, you might be wondering why you would choose to put your child through an experience that threatens to overwhelm their system and has the potential to create additional stress. You might also be wondering how you are going to manage watching their little brain and body experience the pain of trying to recall traumatic experiences. After all, processing trauma memories is one of the toughest parts of therapy because it requires the child to *feel* some part of these memories all over again. This is difficult work, which is why they need the safe container of a therapeutic parent sitting beside them. Although it can be difficult to urge your child to move toward something that you know will cause them to feel pain, there are three reasons why it's better to help them process trauma memories as early as possible.

The first is that it gets harder to process memories the longer they are stored away. Think about this in terms of the layers of an onion. For a four-year-old child who has experienced trauma, there are four years of layers on top of their experiences. However, for a forty-four-year-old adult, there are forty-four years of layers on top of their early trauma. The density of these layers directly relates to the difficulty they have in accessing their core memories. By the time someone is an adult, they have developed many protective and dissociative responses to avoid recalling the trauma, resulting in well-worn pathways in the brain that are associated with that person's typical behaviors and responses.

The second reason is that when children are young, it is more natural for them to lean on an adult when things get scary. When they no longer have the comforting and co-regulating presence of an adult who can take care of their needs, it is so much more complicated to resolve early childhood trauma. We have supported many young adults whose families believed that when they were older, they would have a better capacity to deal with their early memories. Instead of time making their memories easier to deal with, the pain is just as intense, and they must face it alone.

The third reason is that unprocessed memories often drive behavior and choices, which can lead to children and youth being misunderstood. These unprocessed memories create the material that a child's brain uses to develop core beliefs about themselves, others, and the world. For example, after trauma, a child may develop core beliefs like "I'm unlovable," "I can't trust anyone," and "Bad things will always happen to me." These beliefs, in turn, lead the child to behave in ways that confirm the negative or self-defeating beliefs they hold, serving as a self-fulfilling prophecy of sorts. For example, children who have developed a core belief that they were rejected due to their own failings often crave positive attention and connection, but they behave in ways that push people away—thereby confirming their core belief.

Therefore, it is important that you reconcile the urge to protect your child with their need to heal. When their early memories have been processed, you will be able to see an incredible difference in your child. They will have a lighter presence, they will be able to access their own internal resources, and they will benefit from the relationships around them on a deeper level. Simply put, they can be the person they were always meant to be that was hidden beneath the pain.

CHAPTER 14

Making Informed Decisions: Trauma Therapy and Complementary Interventions

Early childhood trauma impacts so many different aspects of development. It not only affects a child's social-emotional functioning but also their sensory processing, communication skills, and cognitive abilities. Therefore, children in trauma therapy often benefit from additional interventions as well, such as speech-language therapy and occupational therapy (OT), which can address the difficulties they are having in other areas. Yet, for most parents, there just isn't enough time in the day to go to OT, speech-language therapy, and trauma therapy—*and* fit in any remaining doctor's appointments, extracurricular activities, and school requirements on top of that. The sheer magnitude of these needs requires more time and energy than any one person could possess, even a loving and committed parent. In this chapter, we walk you through the decision-making process when considering what complementary interventions may be right for your child.

Prioritizing Family Needs

As the parent of a child with trauma, you are faced with the task of making decisions about what interventions your child needs (and when to access them), all while triaging the needs of everyone else in the family. At times, one child's needs might seem to take precedence, while at other times, shifting circumstances might require you to urgently attend to another family member's needs. Similarly, there may be seasons of life when financial security is the priority, meaning that therapeutic support services must be put on hold. The toughest part is that life just keeps on "life-ing," and your best-laid plans seem to constantly require reorganization. We're sure that, at times, you imagine what it would be like to put someone else in charge to relieve the stress of so much decision-making.

If you are struggling to decide how to prioritize your family's needs, remember from chapter 9 that all families operate as a system. Problems for any one person in the system will cause reverberations throughout the system as a whole. To maintain stability in the system, there must be a stabilizing force, or foundation, upon which it is built—and that foundation is *you*. Without this stabilizing force, all subsequent structures built on top of the system will be shaky. That means it is crucial for you to attend to your own psychological and physical needs first if you want a solid foundation upon which the family system can rest.

You might feel like it is irresponsible to leave your child struggling with the impact of trauma while you attend to your own needs. After all, don't good parents put their children first? The answer is of course, but at the same time, if you neglect your own needs, you will start to lose your capacity to be your family's foundation. Noticing and attending to yourself first sets you and your child up for success. Therefore, you want to make sure that first and foremost, you are meeting your own basic needs (for example, for food, sleep, and movement), attending to the discomfort you feel in your body, and accessing your own emotional support from someone you trust.

Once you have that foundation in place, it's time to start making decisions about what issues your child needs addressed first. It will be impossible to engage in multiple interventions at the same time, nor is it recommended. If you are struggling with the overwhelming weight of trying to fix every problem, remember from chapter 2 that attachment is the building block that allows for healthy development to occur. Practically speaking, that means you need to provide your child with relational experiences that make them feel safe and secure—attuning to their needs, responding with empathy to big behaviors, and soothing them when something is uncomfortable or scary—*before* moving on to interventions that address specific developmental concerns. If you think about it, this makes sense: A child who is not speaking by the age of five will likely need speech-language therapy to help them develop this crucial skill, but if they don't feel safe and connected to their primary attachment figure, their brain won't have the foundation it needs to advance to this next developmental stage.

If you have multiple children's needs to consider, it can be difficult to know who and what to prioritize. We suggest starting with the child who is struggling with the most basic stage of psychosocial development, called the "infancy stage" of development. Children in this stage lack trust in others because their basic needs for comfort, food, and love were previously not met. Your goal is to help your child develop this trust by modeling for them what a safe and secure attachment relationship looks like. (See appendix D for a table of Erik Erikson's stages of development, ranging from infancy to adolescence.) If you have multiple children who are stuck in this stage of development, we suggest starting with the oldest child, as they have experienced the longest deprivation of secure attachment. This can feel a bit harsh when you feel the intense needs of all your children—and of course, all children deserve to have their basic needs met—but it may be impossible to adequately address everyone's needs simultaneously.

Jessica and Zara: Prioritizing Needs and Therapy Interventions

Zara was a four-year-old girl who experienced years of deprivation before being adopted by her current family. Just last week, the pediatrician told Zara's mother, Jessica, that Zara's development was that of a twelve-to-eighteen-month-old in most areas. Jessica had little information to prepare her for the experience of having a child who was behind in all areas of development. She certainly was not prepared for the emotional impact of watching trauma play out in the body and mind of a terrified toddler.

Zara's social worker referred the family to a therapist to help them address her needs. As Jessica shared Zara's story with the therapist, she sighed heavily, cried intermittently, and noted that her chest felt tight and heavy. "It's impossible to know where to start when she needs so much help and I'm only one person." The therapist acknowledged the enormity of Zara's needs and empathized with how overwhelmed Jessica was feeling. She knew Mom needed some support in developing a realistic plan for helping Zara heal, so she walked her through the decision-making process about what to prioritize.

She explained that Jessica first needed to meet Zara's needs for physical comfort in the same way you would for an infant. By predictably responding to this basic need, Zara would start to develop trust in her parents' ability to help her feel safe and calm. This led to the second priority: attachment. By practicing the four steps of therapeutic parenting, Jessica could lay down a foundation of secure attachment that would allow for healthy development. Only once this foundation was laid down could they move forward with interventions that would help Zara develop other skills, such as speech and language, gross and fine motor skills, and independent toileting.

When Jessica realized she could focus on one aspect of healing at a time—starting from the foundation and building up—she regained her confidence and enthusiasm for meeting Zara's needs. She relaxed into the idea that this was a step-by-step journey that would take years, and was able to celebrate the small gains Zara made in each area of development.

Once you have triaged your family's needs and developed a secure base for those who need it, you can move forward with complementary interventions that are targeted toward specific developmental skills. In the following section, we discuss some of these interventions in detail, though the scope of possible interventions is so wide that we are not able to offer a comprehensive introduction to all of them. Rather, we've chosen a few that we've encountered most frequently with the families we work with. These are not listed in any particular order, as different families will need different supports at different times. In addition, not every child will require all these interventions—some will require none and others might require several. We recommend working with your therapist to obtain a thorough assessment of your child's functioning so you can create a well-developed plan that meets the needs of your family and your child.

Complementary Interventions
Safe and Sound Protocol

The safe and sound protocol (SSP) is a listening therapy developed by Dr. Stephen Porges that uses the power of music to calm the nervous system. It is specifically designed for kids who struggle with social-emotional difficulties, auditory sensitivities, inattention, anxiety, and trauma-related challenges (Unyte Health, 2024). The SSP involves listening to uniquely designed music through a set of headphones, which sends a message to your child's nervous system that they are well and safe.

The best part about the SSP is that it doesn't just work when you're listening to the music; it also strengthens the nervous system as a whole in preparation for processing difficult memories. Our clinical experience has been consistent with this as well. We have noticed that when children come into the therapy room feeling anxious about what to expect in session, they respond well to the SSP because nothing is required of them initially. We have also found that parents who are struggling to regulate themselves in session benefit from engaging in the SSP alongside their children, and they find themselves more able to manage their own bodies in sessions.

You can offer families the SSP in your office or direct them to listen to it on their own time. (It is available online at https://integratedlistening.com/products/ssp-safe-sound-protocol.) Sometimes, families are not in a place where they can start attending weekly or even biweekly sessions, but they do have the space to listen to the music for fifteen to thirty minutes each day in the comfort of their own home. This can be an excellent way to work on regulation and attachment skills prior to starting trauma therapy.

Parent-Child Play Therapy

In chapter 8, we discussed the importance of attunement and explored how to better understand your child's view of the world, themself, and others. One parent-child intervention that can help you further develop your attunement skills is called watch, wait, and wonder (WWW; Muir et al., 1999). This dyadic intervention, developed by Nancy Cohen, uses child-directed play as an opportunity for parents to watch their child, wait to be invited into their child's world, and wonder about the inner workings of their child. This play-based therapy also allows kids to unconsciously play out any experiences that they may not have language for. By processing their past experiences through the magic of play, they can obtain relief from the intensity of that memory. Some children can also work through future experiences in this way, predicting what those experiences will feel like and how others might respond.

Another model of parent-child play therapy is child-parent relationship therapy (CPRT; Landreth & Bratton, 2019), which offers more guided and scripted opportunities for parents to use play to understand and respond empathically to their child's experiences. In contrast to WWW, which involves engaging in mindfulness while being with the child, CPRT has a strong educational component in which parents are taught how to respond appropriately to their child's behaviors both during and outside of the play sessions. Both are supportive interventions for parents who need extra guidance on developing the foundational skill of attunement.

Occupational Therapy

OT is a form of therapy that can address a wide range of concerns, including delays in fine motor skills (such as buttoning clothing and writing), gross motor skills (such as balancing, jumping, and coordination), activities of daily living (such as feeding and toileting), sensory processing (such as sensitivities to certain textures or sounds), and more. If you have a child who has struggled to meet pivotal developmental milestones (such as crawling, walking, or sitting) or who struggles with basic tasks like dressing themself, preparing a snack, or engaging appropriately in social situations, then pediatric OT might be a good fit for them.

You can attend OT sessions with your child and implement any prescribed at-home activities with the support of your occupational therapist. No language is required for OT to be effective, which is a bonus for children whose trauma has impacted language development. It's important to remember that OT activities should "feel good" to your child, especially in the early stages of parent-child relationship building. This means you might need to exert a great deal of creativity to find a therapeutic activity that both meets the therapy goal and feels good to the child. For example, if your child is struggling with toileting, you might need to incorporate preferred sensory activities your child can do while they're "waiting" for their body to do its job. This can include having your child's favorite music, books, or action figures easily accessible anytime they use the toilet. By incorporating pleasurable activities into the routines of toileting, the brain and body can organize themselves in a way that reduces discomfort or fear. If your child finds the OT experiences to be uncomfortable, it may interfere with relational safety and security, which is your first point of intervention.

Speech-Language Therapy

Speech-language therapy is designed to help children with a wide range of communication difficulties. It begins with a speech assessment to identify what barriers the child is experiencing in their ability to communicate. The therapist will then use a variety of activities to encourage the child to interact, play, and engage with others through words, gestures, objects, or devices. Speech-language therapy also works with challenges like stuttering and lisps, as it teaches children proper pronunciation, cadence, and articulation. Children who have not had healthy relational experiences early in life, or who've had significant trauma during the developmental period when speech emerges, often struggle to communicate verbally. Speech-language therapy supports them in identifying missed experiences that are foundational to the development of language. Parents are often actively involved in speech-language therapy, as it is helpful to continue the work between sessions.

Neurofeedback

Neurofeedback is a noninvasive therapy that involves using EEG technology to monitor electrical activity in the brain, with the goal of eventually retraining how the brain functions. To begin, the child will settle into a comfortable chair while electrode sensors are placed on their scalp. These electrodes transmit information regarding the child's brain activity to a computer. After the therapist establishes a baseline measure of the child's natural brain wave patterns, the child watches different video-game-like animations on the screen, which can be quite entertaining. The audiovisual cues fade in and out of the screen depending on whether the brain is responding according to a desired frequency. Essentially, the brain learns how to correct itself and stay at a particular target frequency to keep the animations from fading out.

Neurofeedback has been used to treat anxiety, depression, sleep difficulties, inattention, impulsivity, aggression, and more. It also has the potential to reduce symptoms of posttraumatic stress disorder, with recent research showing that twenty-four sessions of neurofeedback significantly reduced trauma symptoms in kids between the ages of six to thirteen (Rogel et al., 2020). In our practice, we have found the outcomes of this intervention to be widely varied; some children experience incredible benefits while others notice very little to no change in functioning. These differences in outcomes might be attributable to the length of the intervention, as more research is needed to determine optimal treatment length.

Psychoeducational Assessment

A psychoeducational assessment is an evaluation intended to identify specific areas of learning where a child might be lacking necessary skills and would benefit from targeted intervention. The assessment process includes a variety of tests and rating scales administered by a psychologist that look at a child's learning style, the way they process information, and their behavioral and emotional development. Looking carefully at why a child is struggling academically ensures that parents can plan for the best way to help their child learn and thrive.

A trauma-informed psychoeducational assessment will consider a child's history and the impact of trauma on their development, ensuring that the outcomes and recommendations will inform an effective plan of intervention. The validity of the results may be influenced by how settled and secure a child feels in their family and relationships. Our observations have led us to believe it is best to wait for approximately one year after any significant life change or traumatic experience before pursuing any psychological assessment.

CONCLUSION

If you've reached the end of this book and still have questions about parent-child trauma therapy, you are in good company. We do too. Our clinical experience tells us that there are endless reactions that children and their families can have to trauma and to the process of healing. We couldn't possibly speak to every issue and every possibility in one book, nor do we have all the answers. Our contribution is a drop in the bucket—a bucket that we hope will continue to fill up over time.

However, if you are a parent, it is our hope that this book has helped you to understand the powerful role that you play in helping your child heal. You now have the tools you need to advocate for your child within and outside of your home as they navigate different spaces and relationships. You provide the protective container that allows your child to safely explore their big hurts. If you are a professional or policymaker, we hope that this book will inspire you to mobilize the resources needed to give families the life-changing experience of parent-child trauma therapy. If you are a therapist, we hope you will continue learning more about how to offer trauma therapy in a way that utilizes the parent as the safe container.

As we were writing this book, we frequently wondered why the writing process felt so weighty and why it seemed so urgent to say all these things—to not miss anything important. Near the end it became clear that we both had this unspoken desire to make sure no one misinterpreted anything we said in a way that might result in a child being harmed. We hold the process of healing trauma with reverence and are constantly in awe of the human brain and body's capacity to heal. We also recognize that therapy can have the potential to cause harm, even when helpers have every intention of making things better. Parent-child trauma therapy is new territory, and we are discovering new insights daily as we continue to support families through the process. We hope that five years from now, we will have a whole new set of insights to share, with the input of our colleagues who are also doing this work as well as that of the families who continue to teach us through their experiences.

REFERENCES

Chambers, J. (2017). The neurobiology of attachment: From infancy to clinical outcomes. *Psychodynamic Psychiatry, 45*(4), 542–563. https://doi.org/10.1521/pdps.2017.45.4.542

Delahooke, M. (2019). *Beyond behaviors: Using brain science and compassion to understand and solve children's behavioral challenges.* PESI Publishing.

Grand, D. (2013). *Brainspotting: The revolutionary new therapy for rapid and effective change.* Sounds True.

Landreth, G. L., & Bratton, S. C. (2019). *Child-parent relationship therapy (CPRT): An evidence-based 10-session filial therapy model* (2nd ed.). Routledge.

Lyons, S., Whyte, K., Stephens, R., & Townsend, H. (2020). *Developmental trauma close up* (2nd ed.). https://beaconhouse.org.uk/wp-content/uploads/2020/02/Developmental-Trauma-Close-Up-Revised-Jan-2020.pdf

Maté, G. (2022). *The myth of normal: Trauma, illness & healing in a toxic culture.* Alfred A. Knopf Canada.

Muir, E., Lojkasek, M., & Cohen, N. (1999). *Watch, wait, and wonder: A manual describing a dyadic infant-led approach to problems in infancy and early childhood.* Hincks-Dellcrest Institute.

Pace, P. (2015). *Lifespan Integration: Connecting ego states through time.* Eirene Imprint.

Perry, B., & Szalavitz, M. (2017). *The boy who was raised by a dog: And other stories from a child psychiatrist's notebook.* Basic Books.

Perry, B., & Winfrey, O. (2021). *What happened to you? Conversations on trauma, resilience, and healing.* Flatiron Books.

Rogel, A., Loomis, A. M., Hamlin, E., Hodgdon, H., Spinazzola, J., & van der Kolk, B. (2020). The impact of neurofeedback training on children with developmental trauma: A randomized controlled study. *Psychological Trauma: Theory, Research, Practice, and Policy, 12*(8), 918–929. https://doi.org/10.1037/tra0000648

Satir, V., Banmen, J., Gerber, J., & Gomori, M. (2006). *The Satir model: Family therapy and beyond*. Science and Behavior Books.

Schwartz, R. (2021). *No bad parts: Healing trauma and restoring wholeness with the internal family systems model*. Sounds True.

Shapiro, F. (2018). *Eye movement desensitization and reprocessing (EMDR) therapy: Basic principles, protocols, and procedures* (3rd ed.). Guilford Press.

Siegel, D. J., & Hartzell, M. (2003). *Parenting from the inside out: How a deeper self-understanding can help you raise children who thrive*. TarcherPerigee.

Unyte Health. (2024). *The safe and sound protocol listening therapy*. https://integratedlistening.com/products/ssp-safe-sound-protocol/

van der Kolk, B. A. (2014). *The body keeps the score: Brain, mind, and body in the healing of trauma*. Penguin Books.

Appendix A

Using Timelines to Understand Complex Behaviors

Note: The numerical timeline is meant to reflect the chronological age of your child.

Step 1: Begin by placing the challenging behavior or missed milestone on the timeline:

In utero 0 1 2 3 4 5 6 7 8 9 10 11 12 13 14 15 16 17 18

Step 2: Identify the stage of development where this skill would optimally have been learned:

In utero 0 1 2 3 4 5 6 7 8 9 10 11 12 13 14 15 16 17 18

Step 3: Identify any life events or traumatic experiences that may have occurred at the same time:

In utero 0 1 2 3 4 5 6 7 8 9 10 11 12 13 14 15 16 17 18

Step 4: Reflections:

_____
_____
_____
_____
_____
_____
_____
_____

Appendix B

A STORY ABOUT GOING TO THERAPY

This is a therapy office where kids and their parents go to play and talk about big feelings.

You and I are going to go together to meet our therapist and learn what happens in therapy. Our therapist's name is Janisa.

Janisa is a safe person. We are going to play and talk with her about some of the things that cause big feelings to happen in our bodies.

When we go inside the therapy office, a lady named Lisa will be there to say hi. She sits at the front desk saying hello and helping people make appointments.

You and I will sit in the waiting area until Janisa is ready to see us. The waiting area has lots of books for us to read and some paper and pencils for coloring.

When we go inside the therapy room with Janisa, we will talk and play with some toys that she has on the floor. Remember, we are going to do this together. You won't be alone at any time.

When we are finished playing and talking, you and I will leave together. Afterward, we will go and eat a snack at your favorite place. Sometimes, you will feel tired, so I will help you.

To be continued...

Appendix C

Daily Noticing Checklist

Use this checklist every day to help you fine-tune your noticing skills.

When was it the most difficult to be with your child today? What behaviors occurred? How was your child feeling then?

_____

_____

_____

What did you notice about your child's body movements today? Were they purposeful, hesitant, energetic, sluggish, nervous, or repetitive? Did you notice any changes? When?

_____

_____

_____

Were there times today when your child tried to get physically close to you? How did they do this? How did it feel for you?

_____

_____

_____

Copyright © 2025 Andrea Chatwin & Meagan VanDiermen,
Healing Big Hurts. All rights reserved.

What behavior was your child using today to express their needs? How did they feel about their own behavior? How did you feel?

_____
_____
_____

What did you notice about your child's facial expressions? When did these change suddenly? What was happening at the time?

_____
_____
_____

What were the circumstances or experiences your child had prior to having a tantrum, a meltdown, a defiant response, or aggression?

_____
_____
_____

When did you notice your child withdrawing from an activity, experience, or relational interaction? What was happening in their body? What might they have been thinking or feeling?

_____
_____
_____

Appendix D

Erikson's Stages of Development

Stage	Basic Conflict	Important Events	Outcomes
Infancy (birth to 18 months)	Trust vs. mistrust	Feeding	Children develop a sense of trust when caregivers provide reliability, care, and affection. A lack of this will lead to mistrust.
Early childhood (2–3 years)	Autonomy vs. shame and doubt	Toilet training	Children will develop a sense of personal control over physical skills and a sense of independence. Success leads to feelings of autonomy. Failure results in feelings of shame and doubt.
Preschool (3–5 years)	Initiative vs. guilt	Exploration	Children need to begin asserting control and power over the environment. Success in this stage leads to a sense of purpose. Children who try to exert too much power experience disapproval, resulting in a sense of guilt.
School age (6–11 years)	Industry vs. inferiority	School	Children need to cope with new school and academic demands. Success leads to a sense of competence, while failure results in feelings of inferiority.
Adolescence (12–18 years)	Identity vs. role confusion	Social relationships	Teens need to develop a sense of self and personal identity. Success leads to an ability to stay true to oneself, while failure leads to role confusion and a weak sense of self.

ABOUT THE AUTHORS

ANDREA CHATWIN, MA, CCC, is the founder and director of A Child's Song Support Services, a multiservice agency that supports families joined together through adoption, foster care, and other forms of permanency. Andrea holds a master's degree in counseling psychology with expertise in early childhood mental health and developmental trauma. She has specialized training as a trauma therapist and has spent over twenty years working with families of children and youth who have had parental or caregiver losses and placement disruptions. Her work on attachment and trauma-informed transitioning of children from care to permanency has resulted in systemic changes.

She is the adoptive parent of two daughters who are now young adults and has therefore experienced firsthand the unique joys and challenges of parenting children who have experienced trauma.

Andrea is the author of two manuals, *Teaching the Hurt Child: Relationships Between Trauma, Attachment and Learning* and *Transitioning Children from Foster Care to Adoption*, as well as two children's books, *My Baby Brain Is Loud Tonight* and *Mabel's Moving*. She has developed programs, presented workshops, and consulted extensively with government agencies, school districts, and nonprofits to support trauma- and attachment-informed responding to children and youth.

MEAGAN VANDIERMEN, MA, RCC, is the clinical director of A Child's Song Support Services, where she supervises a team of clinical counselors in providing trauma therapy to children and families who have been joined together through adoption, foster care, and other forms of permanency. Meagan holds a master's degree in counseling psychology and has specific training in Observed Experiential

Integration (OEI) and Lifespan Integration (LI) therapy, two dynamic body-based trauma interventions that are effective in working with people of all ages to provide deep healing. Meagan's over fifteen years of experience in providing trauma therapy has led to expertise in treating preverbal trauma while simultaneously enhancing the therapeutic nature of the parent-child relationship.

Meagan is actively involved in research that seeks to find the most efficient and meaningful processes that promote healing for families who have challenges in accessing services. She is passionate about offering cutting-edge, science-based information through workshops and trainings for school and government professionals to further their understanding of trauma-informed care.

Meagan credits her experiences working in orphanages overseas with her developing a passion for treating children who have experienced caregiver disruptions and other relational trauma. Meagan resides in Vancouver, British Columbia, with her husband and four children.